The Prime Minister

and Cabinet

Books in the Politics Study Guides series

The Prime Minister and Cabinet

Stephen Buckley

Edinburgh University Press

This book is dedicated to the memory of my father,
Ronald Buckley, 1927–2002

© Stephen Buckley, 2006

Edinburgh University Press Ltd
22 George Square, Edinburgh

Typeset in 11/13pt Monotype Baskerville by
Servis Filmsetting Ltd, Manchester, and
printed and bound in Great Britain by
Antony Rowe Ltd, Chippenham, Wilts

A CIP record for this book is available from the British Library

ISBN-10 0 7486 2289 6 (paperback)
ISBN-13 978 0 7486 2289 4 (paperback)

The right of Stephen Buckley to be identified as author of this work has been
asserted in accordance with the Copyright, Designs and Patents Act 1988.

Published with the support of the Edinburgh University Scholarly
Publishing Initiatives Fund

Contents

Boxes

Tables

Acknowledgements

This book is the product of more than ten years of conversations and discussions with a steadily growing number of A-level students. There are now too many of you to list, but you know who you are, and your teacher thanks you from across the years. I should like to acknowledge a greater (and long overdue) debt of honour to the Department of Politics and Contemporary History at the University of Salford for all the initial encouragement in the study and teaching of politics. More recently, I should like to thank the Politics Association, especially the tireless work and encouragement of Glynis Sandwith and the PARC editor, Duncan Watts, who edited this volume with equal measures of enthusiasm and patience. I never come away from a conversation with Duncan feeling anything other than inspired and supported. Pauline Rees, Jacqui Wood, Vanessa Pryce, Jackie Cahalin, Ed Elvish, Lance Edynbry and Nicola Ramsey at Edinburgh University Press have all helped in different ways at different times – thank you. Finally, thanks are due to my family, both in Oldham and in Barrow but especially to my wife Caroline and our children Amelia and Will.

Introduction

The central executive territory of the British system of government is an exciting, dramatic and highly complex area of modern politics. This book is designed to satisfy A-level students and university undergraduates who are seeking a single-volume approach to this particular aspect of their political studies.

This book seeks to illustrate a central point about the modern system of government and governance in the United Kingdom – that the Prime Minister and Cabinet now represent the central element of a core **system** of government made up of a complex and complicated network of relationships, alliances and resource partnerships. While the Prime Minister and the Cabinet are essential components of this system, they are not always able to dominate and control the way it functions. They must work to accommodate the aims and ambitions of other agencies while, at the same time, responding to the unpredictable and rapidly changing contexts of domestic and international circumstances that are, to misquote Dickens's Mr Micawber, 'beyond their individual control'.

The book begins with an overview of the executive territory that introduces the key structures, concepts, theories and histories of the executive branch of British government. All the discussions that take place in the remaining nine chapters are set initially in context as part of this opening chapter.

Chapter 2 charts the origins, role and structure of the British cabinet system of government and will provide details of the make-up of the modern Cabinet prior to discussing the traditional and constitutional roles of modern cabinet government. Cabinet hierarchies and the selection and removal of cabinet ministers will also be covered here.

Chapter 3 will continue to look at the Cabinet but will focus on the bureaucracy of the cabinet system. We shall examine the development of cabinet committees, the use of cabinet committees by recent Prime Ministers and effectiveness of cabinet committees. We shall also consider the structure and role of the Cabinet Office and the structure and role of the Cabinet Secretariat under Tony Blair. The chapter will conclude with a discussion of the recent reforms to the workings and structure of the Cabinet Office.

Definitions and traditional views of how the doctrine of collective responsibility came into being will be discussed in Chapter 4 as will the impact of recent events, especially those surrounding the war in Iraq, on the condition of cabinet government. This will lead into a detailed introduction to the debate surrounding the 'decline' of cabinet government which will be developed in more detail in later chapters when the focus is on prime ministerial power.

Attention turns to the Prime Minister in Chapter 5 with a discussion of prime ministerial power and the constraints on the powers of the Prime Minister. Chapter 6 will develop the discussion to focus on the support and bureaucracy of the Prime Minister and will include analysis of the role of Downing Street, wider means of prime ministerial support and a case study of the role of Lord Birt. The chapter will also look at trends in prime ministerial support, and will consider the question: should there be a Prime Minister's Department?

The debate on the nature of prime ministerial style and why the study of prime ministerial style is important is the focus of Chapter 7. The distinction between style and personality and political style as political skill will be discussed before comparing the political styles of Margaret Thatcher, John Major and Tony Blair.

Chapter 8 – 'Hail to the Chief?' – will consider the extent to which the Prime Minister is, or is in the process of becoming, a presidential type of leader, and will provide an overview of the debate surrounding the issue of prime ministerial versus presidential government. Arguments here will be illustrated with examples from the prime ministerial careers of Margaret Thatcher and Tony Blair. The arguments for and against presidentialism will be outlined, as will the key arguments of Michael Foley.

The 'core executive' analysed in Chapter 9 brings together all the key elements and conclusions of the book. The 'core executive' refers to the key institutions at the very centre of a system of government. It consists of a large and variable number of players that includes the Prime Minister, the Cabinet and its committees, the Prime Minister's Office and the Cabinet Office. It also includes large co-ordinating departments such as the government's law officers, the security and intelligence services and the Treasury. We will look at definitions and theories of the nature of core executives, the nature of prime ministerial / civil servant relationships in a core executive and the changing context of prime ministerial influence. We will also look at how the core executive works and how it has evolved before considering some of the criticisms of the core executive.

Finally, the concluding Chapter 10 will bring together the key arguments of the book and will suggest ways in which students may wish to use the other books in this series to undertake a detailed synoptic overview of the Prime Minister and Cabinet in terms of other aspects of the British political system, and even perhaps to consider using the information and arguments here as a starting point for detailed comparative study.

The chapters in this book focus on the British executive at a crucial point in its history. This fact is illustrated by the following points, all relevant in the summer of 2005:

- A Labour leader/Prime Minister recently returned to power in an historical third election victory.
- A Prime Minister who has announced his intention to retire before the next general election.
- An obvious 'leader in waiting' in the shape of Gordon Brown.
- A European Union in political turmoil following the rejection of the Constitutional Treaty.
- The continued presence of British armed forces in Iraq with no obvious sign of an 'exit strategy'.
- Terrorist attacks on London by suicide bombers and subsequent anti-terrorist measures that raised some issues of civil liberties.

The sheer complexity of the situations listed above defy any simplistic attempts by politicians to deal with them in anything like the 'traditional' and 'constitutional' ways beloved of those who cling to an essentially nineteenth-century view of how the central executive should be arranged.

As we have already said, the modern political world is complex and complicated, and the political relationships that develop within it are a product of that complexity and confusion. As far as the United Kingdom is concerned, the traditional view of a neat machine at the heart of a government based on collective Cabinet responsibility no longer applies. This is now government by complex and interwoven webs of relationships, networks and contacts. How much of this is actually controlled by the politicians enmeshed inside it is a question for which there are no simple answers.

CHAPTER 1

The Executive Territory

Contents

Overview

The opening chapter examines the central branch of government that will form the basis of the rest of the book – the executive. By choosing to focus on executive power and executive territory in its broadest sense, a firm grounding will be established on which to construct a much more detailed analysis of the central executive territory in the British system of parliamentary democracy.

Key issues to be covered in this chapter

- Defining the executive
- Defining the Cabinet
- Defining the Prime Minister
- Summary of the positions of heads of state and heads of government
- Comparing parliamentary and presidential systems
- The relationship between the executive and the legislature

Introduction

To develop a full understanding of the role, place and importance of the **Prime Minister** and **Cabinet** in the modern British system of government, it becomes necessary to place both institutions in the wider context of executive powers and territories in Western liberal democracies. Having established a clear set of guidelines as to the nature of modern executive power we can go on to construct a detailed analysis of Cabinet and Prime Minister.

Defining the executive

In this section we shall begin by defining the executive before going on to provide clear definitions of:

- Cabinet
- Prime Minister
- Heads of state and heads of government

This section will also provide a brief comparison of parliamentary and presidential systems.

If we attempt to locate the centre of political power and authority in a state we usually find it in the **executive** branch of government. It is the role of the executive to organise and arrange the affairs of the nation state by formulating and then implementing policy decisions. The work of the executive is usually performed by two distinct groups of people:

- elected politicians
- paid, permanent officials (such as the Civil Service in the United Kingdom)

It is this political control of the state's affairs by the executive that we refer to as **government**. The terms 'executive' and 'government' therefore become interchangeable. In the United Kingdom, the government consists of the chief or head of the executive – the Prime Minister – plus his or her chosen Cabinet and junior ministers. Other political systems organise their executives in similar ways.

- In the United States the President is the chief executive and chooses the Cabinet. Cabinet posts in the US, however, are filled by unelected individuals.
- Germany has a parliamentary head of government, or prime minister, called the Chancellor. The Chancellor is chosen by a majority of the popularly elected lower house of parliament, the *Bundestag* (Federal Assembly). The Chancellor then selects a Cabinet of about twenty ministers from among the parties in the *Bundestag* to form what is usually a coalition government.
- The government in Japan is headed by a Prime Minister who appoints the Cabinet.
- The head of government in Turkey is a Prime Minister who appoints the Cabinet.
- Spain, a constitutional monarchy like the United Kingdom, is headed by a President of the government (basically a prime minister). The monarch appoints cabinet ministers on the recommendation of the prime minister.
- Sweden, another monarchy, has a Prime Minister who appoints his or her Cabinet.
- Finally, in France, the head of the government is the Prime Minister, who is appointed by the President. The Council of Ministers (Cabinet) is appointed by the Prime Minister.

The notion of the modern executive was given its most influential interpretation by the eighteenth-century French political theorist, Charles Louis de Secondat, Baron de Montesquieu. Montesquieu was observing the system of government in pre-Revolutionary France. In 1748, in his book *The Spirit of Laws*, he first put forward the theory of **separation of powers**. The French state at this time was ruled by the monarchy, and Louis XIV had emphasised the power that lay in his hands by referring to himself as 'the state' – '*L'état c'est moi*'. Therefore, in eighteenth-century France, Louis was laying claim to be, in one person, the living embodiment of the legislature, the executive and the judiciary.

In *The Spirit of Laws*, Montesquieu questioned the absolute power of the rulers of France by making a case for a 'separation of powers' based on the principle that the legislature, executive and judiciary be ordered in such a way as to be three independent and separated branches of government. Organise a government on these lines, argued Montesquieu, and each branch will check and balance the other, thus maintaining a democratic system, freedom of the individual and offer protection against tyrannical power that places the whole state in the hands of one person. If the three branches of government are not separated, then liberty is lost.

In the United States, this principle of separation of powers has been a central doctrine of the Constitution since its framing in 1789. In British politics, however, the principle is less clear. The key factor to keep in mind when observing and comparing separation of powers in the two systems is the respective constitutions. Compared against the rigid and written American Constitution the British Constitution is uncodified and has evolved over time as opposed to being fixed at a clear starting point in history. This evolution has allowed the three branches of government in Britain to overlap, become blurred and in some cases 'fuse' together.

Table 1.1 attempts to clarify these three roles and to show how they operate in the United Kingdom and the United States.

Two key points need to be re-emphasised in relation to the table – first, the written American constitution clearly establishes the principle of extensive separation of powers (as opposed to the uncodified United Kingdom Constitution); and, second, as we have already mentioned, several aspects of the British system have become 'fused'. This fusion is illustrated in Table 1.2.

Having established a basic definition of executive power we need to look closely at its application in the British system of government.

The Cabinet

The Cabinet dominates the executive branch of government in Britain. Britain is therefore traditionally said to have **cabinet government** made up of a relatively small group of MPs drawn from the legislature and headed by the Prime Minister. The Cabinet is traditionally said to operate as a decision-making body, to provide an opportunity for the general management over the formulation of policy, and to give some clear cohesion to the programme on which the government has been elected. In doing this, the structure of the Cabinet should allow all departmental perspectives and competing claims to be filtered through the specific issue being debated. It is this

Table 1.1 The separation of powers in the UK and the USA		
The element	**UK**	**USA**
Legislature – passes and, in some cases, makes the law.	• Parliament – the House of Commons and the House of Lords. • Passes more law on behalf of the executive than it makes itself.	• Congress – Senate and the House of Representatives. • Has more opportunity to pass laws of its own than the UK Parliament.
Executive – those who are responsible for making the day-by-day decisions on how the country should be governed.	• The Crown, the Cabinet, The Prime Minister and ministers, and the Civil Service. • Also includes some local and regional government and needs to take account of UK membership of the EU.	• The President and those individuals chosen by the President to be part of the Cabinet.
Judiciary – where laws put forward by the executive and passed by the legislature are interpreted and enforced.	• The judicial system and the hierarchy of courts.	• The Supreme Court that acts as the guardian of the Constitution

process, particularly the quality of the debates and discussions, that, in recent years, has been subject to close scrutiny by those who feel that Cabinet has drifted away from what was its traditional role. For some people, this is nothing less than the decline of cabinet government, and will be discussed at length later in this book. Nevertheless,

Table 1.2 The UK: a separation of powers or fusion?

The Prime Minister	• Head of the executive, yet is elected to represent a constituency in Parliament (the legislature) and regularly attends sessions in the Commons.
	Compare this with
	• The American President is elected to be head of the executive. The President has no part to play in the day-to-day business of Congress.
The Cabinet	• Similar to the Prime Minister in that most cabinet ministers will be MPs elected to represent a constituency in the Commons. They are therefore in the executive *and* the legislature.
	Compare this with
	• The Presidential Cabinet in the US which is appointed, not elected, and which has no role in the business of Congress.
The Lord Chancellor	• The leading Law officer in the UK.
	• Appointed by the Prime Minister.
	• Member of the Cabinet.
	• Speaker in the House of Lords.
	• The most senior judge in the judiciary.
	• The lord Chancellor is probably unique in that he manages to be a member of all three branches of government.
	• Law lords also find themselves in both the legislature and the judiciary.

in broad terms, cabinet government remains the collective expression of the executive. The origins of the Cabinet, and an overview of the constitutional struggles with the monarchy, will be discussed in Chapter 2. For now, we offer a broad analysis of the principles of cabinet government.

The Cabinet has been traditionally viewed as playing a crucial role in the democratic system, accountable to Parliament for the actions of government departments and ministers and providing, in the memorable phrase of the nineteenth-century political writer, Walter Bagehot, 'the efficient secret of the English constitution . . . the close union, the nearly complete fusion, of the executive and legislative powers . . . A cabinet is a combining committee – a hyphen which joins, a buckle which fastens, the legislative part of the state to the executive part of the state.' In practice, however, the role of the cabinet in the unwritten constitution has always been informal. If we go back and examine the origins of cabinet government around the time of the 1688 **Glorious Revolution** we will see that the Cabinet was given no legal powers, no formal status. Whatever powers the Cabinet might be said to hold have always been those given to the individual ministers by the Crown and not to the Cabinet in any collective way.[1]

For some observers, the constitutional vagueness on which the Cabinet rests is a cause for concern. While arguing that the Cabinet is 'a self-moderating form of government which protects against tyranny and is quite different from the dictatorial, presidential or monarchical systems found in many countries of the world and throughout history', John Kingdom goes on to argue that it is only convention that ensures that cabinet government will take place, and that these particular conventions, though supremely important, are among the most fragile in the Constitution.[2] Kingdom's arguments, especially those relating to the lack of constitutional constraints on the executive, and the suggestions that the real power of the executive lies not in the Cabinet but elsewhere, will be examined in detail in later chapters. It is enough for now, in this general introduction to executive power, to point the way to these later debates and to emphasise their importance.

The Prime Minister chairs the modern Cabinet. It will be the Prime Minister who will select those Members of Parliament who will sit in the Cabinet and who will eventually reshuffle them around the cabinet table or sack them. Most cabinet members have the title 'Secretary of State' and will be given responsibility for managing a Department of State, or 'Ministry'.

We have already made the point that the constitutional position of the Cabinet is, at best, vague and that the Cabinet as such has no legal powers. What powers the Cabinet may be said to have are actually those vested in its members as secretaries of state. It is only the doctrine of collective cabinet responsibility that binds all members of the cabinet to support the decisions taken in cabinet meetings. Failure to do this usually results in resignation or the sack. We will examine the doctrine of collective cabinet responsibility in more detail in Chapter 3.

Cabinet functions will be covered in depth elsewhere but for now may be briefly summarised as follows:

- Deciding the main directions of domestic and foreign policy.
- Controlling the agenda in Parliament.
- Co-ordinating the policies of government departments.
- Allocating the expenditure of government
- Long-term strategic planning.
- 'Troubleshooting' unforeseen difficulties and problems.

For the Cabinet to be able to carry out the growing workload of government effectively, a system of **cabinet committees** has been developing steadily since its introduction in 1916. Although the existence of cabinet committees was only officially recognised in 1992, the network of committees has broadened into three main groups: committees, subcommittees and ministerial groups. These committees and groups now form a significant part of the cabinet system and will be discussed in detail when we look more closely at the Cabinet and when we address the issues and questions surrounding the supposed decline of cabinet government.

Given the scale of what we have already described, it should come as no surprise to discover that the modern Cabinet requires a substantial bureaucracy to help with the growing amount of administration. Since 1916, the business of the Cabinet – its agendas, discussions, decisions and minutes – has been the responsibility of a **cabinet office** headed by a cabinet secretary. At the time of writing the cabinet secretary was Andrew Turnbull and, as such, he held the position of the most senior civil servant in the United Kingdom. Turnbull retired in the summer of 2005 and was replaced by Sir Gus O'Donnell.

The Cabinet Office is based in 10 Downing Street from where it organises every aspect of the work of Cabinet and its numerous subcommittees and groups. As we shall soon discover, the various duties of the Cabinet Office and its official committees can often be interpreted in an overtly political and non-neutral manner. Given the nature of cabinet minutes, and the fact that they are drawn up by the Cabinet Secretary in consultation with the Prime Minister, some ministers frequently question the extent to which the minutes of a cabinet meeting have been written more to reflect the wishes of the Prime Minister than being an accurate record of what took place in the meeting. As we will go on to illustrate, it is possible to see the Cabinet Office as having a clearly political role at the heart of the executive.

As we shall see, not everyone can agree on what position the Cabinet now occupies in the executive. Views range from the gloomy prognosis of the 'death' of cabinet government through to the more realistic arguments surrounding 'systems' of cabinet government and beyond to the views of those who argue in favour of the centre of the executive being dominated by a flexible and changing 'core' of key players enmeshed in a complex system of relationships.

The Prime Minister

The position of the Prime Minister is similar to that of the Cabinet in that it has no clear constitutional role. Nevertheless, the office of Prime Minister is now undoubtedly at the very heart of the executive and, as such, holds substantial political power. Because of the vague nature of the Constitution on the position of the Prime Minister, and because of the particular way that the position has evolved, there are substantial and far-reaching powers now associated with the office that are not always immediately obvious simply by observing the 'official' powers.

It is this 'evolution' of prime ministerial power that we will examine in some detail in Chapter 4. Similarly to that which has already been said here about the Cabinet, it is important to remember the lack of clear constitutional structure around the post of prime minister. Having evolved as a result of a 'Hanoverian lack of Kingly interest in all things British',[3] the post of prime minister quickly developed in order to fill the power vacuum that the monarch had left in the Cabinet. There is, in this evolution of power, an interesting historical irony. The office of prime minister, certainly by the early nineteenth-century at least, had assumed a superior if not supreme position in relation to the rest of the Cabinet. The whole point of the struggles between Parliament and the Crown in the late eighteenth-century had been about the overbearing political power of the monarch. What the architects of the Glorious Revolution of 1688 had not intended was that the power and position of the monarch would simply be rewritten and reconstituted through the prime minister almost as a kind of 'popular' monarchy.

In this introductory overview of the British executive it is necessary to raise the issue of the 'Prime Minister as President' debate in order to highlight the detailed discussions elsewhere in this book and to offer a brief attempt at a general comparison of heads of executives. To a certain extent, the debate surrounding prime ministerial power has moved on substantially since the early days of the prime minister versus president arguments. Cabinet 'systems' and 'core' executives are two schools of study that offer us greater insight into the true nature of prime ministerial power than was necessarily the case as recently as the mid-1990s.

Head of state, head of government

When considering the nature of executive power it is useful to have made the clear distinction between 'state' and 'government' beforehand. We have already explained the nature of government as embodied in the élite group who have the authority to make laws and to run the state – but what is the state?

It is often useful to think of the state as all the things that would remain if the government as a group of elected individuals were to be abducted by aliens some time next week. The politicians may be gone, yet the institutions and central concepts of the state would remain. The United Kingdom would presumably retain its territory and borders, the citizens (or subjects) of the state would also remain, as would the idea of a British nation sharing a set of broad similarities in terms of language, culture, history and values. Law and order, the authority we give to the police, the acceptance of a limited monarchy and the central institutions of government would remain also. It would no doubt be the case that a new government would be constituted and assume control over and within the Constitution and that Parliament would still be sovereign – the highest law-making authority in the land. Governments organise and order the workings of the state. Those governments will come and they will go. The state remains. The problem in the United Kingdom, as we shall now show, is never this simple. The line between 'state' and 'government' is never clear, and the powers of the monarch and prime minister in relation to the state and government can be equally confusing.

In the United kingdom the monarch is the formal head of state. When power was transferred from the monarch to the executive at the end of the eighteenth century, it allowed a distinction to be made between head of state and head of government. As we shall see, however, this distinction is not always clear. *possesses*.

The main powers that the Prime Minister has at his or her disposal are known as **prerogative powers** and are derived from those functions that, before 1688, were performed by the monarchy. This constitutional convention (there are no statutes or legal rulings that confirm this state of affairs) allows the Prime Minister to carry out functions in the name of the monarchy even though the crown plays no active part in them. Part of these prerogative powers are performed by the current Prime Minister on behalf of the Queen as head of state as opposed to those that Tony Blair will find himself performing as head of government.

In those political systems based on republican, as opposed to limited monarchy, doctrines, the powers of the head of state would normally be carried out by an elected president and would be outside the arena of party politics and would therefore be performed on behalf of the whole nation. Those duties that do have a party political aspect are normally carried out by a head of government, either by a prime minister or some such equivalent. The only other established democracy that accepts this dual role of head of state and head of government is the United States. In France, Germany, Ireland and most other western democracies, the distinction between head of state and head of government is clear and makes the comparison with the Prime Minister of the United Kingdom more stark, especially as the British Prime Minister does not usually make it clear in which capacity he or she is operating. In this sense, Margaret Thatcher's description of her meetings with the American President as being that of 'two heads of state' at least clarified the issue for her, irrespective of the constitutional questions it raised. Having raised the issue of distinctions between heads of state and government in relation to our discussions on executive power we shall leave the debate and return to it later in the book.

Relations between the executive and the legislature

Having established a basic set of definitions of the executive around the Cabinet and the Prime Minister it will be useful to our later discussions of executive power in the United Kingdom if we outline some key points that are relative to the nature of the relationship between the executive and the **legislature**. In this section we will introduce the following areas for discussion:

- Cabinet and Parliament
- Prime Minister and Parliament
- The executive and the European Union

The relationship between the executive and the legislature in a political system is crucial to how that system will operate and govern in practice. The United Kingdom has **parliamentary government**. Here, the personnel of the executive are drawn from, and may be located in, the legislature. In a parliamentary system the government is held to be collectively accountable to the legislature for the decisions that it makes and will remain in office only for the time that it can retain the confidence of that body. Australia has this form of government, as does New Zealand. Not surprisingly, because the United Kingdom was a major influence on its post-war re-structuring, Germany may be said to have many of the features normally associated with parliamentary government, apart from the crucial difference by which members of the German Cabinet are not required to be members of the German legislature – the *Bundestag*.

Alternatively, some executives are part of presidential systems of government. In this system the executive and the legislature are composed of two separate groups of people. As we have already shown, the President of the United States is elected for a four-year term of office. The election for the President is separate from those elections that choose members to sit in the two houses of Congress. The President and the members of his Cabinet are prohibited from being members of the Congress by the American Constitution.

Not all liberal democracies organise the relationship between the executive and the legislature on a strictly parliamentary or presidential basis. France, for instance, has a hybrid form of government that combines features that are both presidential and parliamentary.

In its strictest sense, the phrase 'legislature' describes those institutions in a political system that make or pass law. In the United Kingdom these functions are carried out by the two chambers of Parliament at Westminster and tend on the whole to be concerned more with passing than with making laws. There are interesting comparisons to be made here between the legislative arrangements in Britain with those of other systems, most notably the United States.

Cabinet and Parliament

The majority of Cabinet members are drawn from the ranks of those members of the winning party in a general election who have been elected to represent constituencies for that party in the House of Commons. The rules governing membership of the Cabinet are once again based on constitutional conventions as opposed to strict rules of statute. This looseness has allowed prime ministers to promote individuals to the Cabinet who have not been elected to serve in the House of Commons. Lord Young served in the Thatcher Cabinet between 1987 and 1988, while Lord Carrington had been Foreign Secretary in an earlier Thatcher Cabinet in the early 1980s and had held a Cabinet position for the Ministry of Defence under Heath during the first half of the 1970s.

The Cabinet has a **collective responsibility** to the United Kingdom Parliament. This collective ministerial responsibility is one of the key features of parliamentary systems of government. Under this convention the supremacy of the legislature is emphasised by its ability to demand the resignation of the government if confidence in that body is lost. This convention does not apply to presidential forms of government because in most cases, the members of the executive are not drawn from the legislature. The extent to which this doctrine remains a central aspect of the British Constitution will be an issue this book looks at in more detail in Chapter 3.

The other key convention governing the relationship between the executive and Parliament is the doctrine of **individual ministerial responsibility**. In brief, the convention of individual ministerial responsibility requires each cabinet minister to be responsible to Parliament for his or her own personal conduct, the general conduct of his or her department, and the actions of his or her civil servants in terms of policy-related actions or omissions. The most important consequence of this convention is that the minister is answerable to Parliament for the work of his or her department. Some prefer to interpret this as Parliament having the power to force the resignation of a minister who has been considered negligent. We should perhaps remind ourselves at this point that the Cabinet has no formal powers other than those invested in its individual members as secretaries of state.

In recent years the key debate relating to the Cabinet and Parliament has been dominated by discussions around the extent to which the executive is able to dominate the legislature. As we shall see, this domination is possible for a number of reasons:

- A highly effective system of government whips in the Commons ensures that, in most cases, back-benchers vote in the way that is expected of them.
- The British system of first past the post encourages large government majorities and so therefore produces parties in Parliament capable of dominating business irrespective of the opposition.
- The payroll vote ensures that junior members of the government would effectively destroy any higher ministerial career if they were ever to vote against the government.

The Prime Minister and Parliament

In the United Kingdom, the Prime Minister is the head of government, exercising many of the executive functions nominally vested in the sovereign, who is head of state. According to custom, the Prime Minister and the Cabinet (which he or she heads) are responsible for their actions to Parliament, of which they are members by (modern) convention. The Prime Minister at the time of writing is Tony Blair, leader of the Labour Party, who has been in office since 1997.

The Prime Minister has been a member of the House of Commons since the early days of the twentieth-century. Sir Alec Douglas-Home, who was Prime Minister for a brief period after the Profumo scandal in the early 1960s, was the first person to renounce his peerage in order to re-enter the House of Commons to lead a party and secure a brief tenure of office. Other than this, you would need to go back to the premiership of Lord Salisbury (1886–1902) to find a Prime Minister who assumed the office directly from the House of Lords.

The House of Commons has the power to act as a check on the powers of the Prime Minister. As head of government the Prime Minister requires the continued support of the House of Commons. Without this support, expressed mainly by the continued goodwill of the party that he or she leads, it is increasingly difficult for the Prime Minister to remain in power. The Prime Minister therefore gets a substantial proportion of his or her authority through the continued support of the House of Commons. As we shall see, the House of Commons checks the powers of the Prime Minister mostly through committee hearings and through question time, a weekly event where the Prime Minister is required to respond to the questions of the leader of the Opposition and other MPs.

The Prime Minister has a slightly different relationship with the House of Lords. Under the Salisbury Convention (1915), the Lords does not normally seek to oppose any measure that is promised by the government in its election manifesto. When the House of Lords does oppose the Prime Minister, it is generally ineffectual in defeating entire bills (though almost all bills are successfully modified by the Upper House during their passage through Parliament).

Peers (members of the House of Lords) are created by the sovereign on the advice of the Prime Minister; by obtaining the creation of several new peers, the Prime Minister may flood the House of Lords with individuals who will support his or her position. Such a tactic was threatened in 1911 to ensure the passage of the Parliament Act which, together with the Parliament Act of 1949, reduce the powers of the House of Lords and establish the supremacy of the Commons (in particular, the House of Lords can only delay, but not reject, most bills on which the Commons insists). Challenges during 2004–5 by the Countryside Alliance on the legality of the Parliament Act were not successful.

It has been argued that recent prime ministers have shown a healthy disdain for Parliament, especially the routine business of the House of Commons. Margaret Thatcher's style in the Commons was 'robust' and 'uncompromising' while Blair's reforms to question time have caused some critics to ask how seriously he takes his responsibilities in relation to the Commons. The system of Prime Minister's Questions (PMQs), for instance, was reformed by Blair shortly after coming to power in May 1997. Previously, PMQs had taken place on Tuesday and Thursday afternoons. Under the new arrangements of question time the leader of the Opposition may make up to six interventions (previously three) and the leader of the Liberal Democrats will normally ask two questions (previously one). This change has prompted much debate. At the time of the change the Conservatives opposed the move claiming it reduced the number of times the Prime Minister was forced to account for his actions in Parliament.

It is generally accepted, then, that in most circumstances, the modern Prime Minister has substantial devices and opportunities which allow him or her to give a clear impression that he or she is, indeed, dominating Parliament. It is not possible to argue, as it is in the case of the United States Congress, that Parliament is always able to exert the same pressure on the Prime Minister as Congress frequently does on the President. Unlike American presidents, British prime ministers have a number of means at their disposal by which they can frequently dominate the legislature for significant periods of time, not least because they are themselves members of the legislature and dominate the party with the largest majority. Other means of executive dominance of Parliament that will be discussed in this book include:

- Control of the Parliamentary timetable
- The opportunity to dominate debate
- The power to dissolve Parliament
- The timing of the general election

Each of the above factors needs to be examined in detail to give a clear account of the arguments surrounding the executive 'dominance' of the legislature in the British system of government. As we shall point out throughout this book, however, the all-embracing nature of the executive can often be overstated and, for every example of executive 'dominance', there remains the potential for the legislature to exercise significant restraint and control.

The executive and the European Union

The traditional role of the United Kingdom executive has changed considerably in the period since Britain became a member of the European Union. Since 1974, the Cabinet is no longer the key decision-making body in respect of any policy area which falls under the jurisdiction of the European Union. Important policy areas, such as agricultural support, consumer protection, the environment, international transport, workers' rights and trade are all covered by European Union legislation. In this context, the **European Council of Ministers** becomes the key body, and it is here that Britain is represented by appropriate cabinet ministers according to the policy area being discussed.

When attending meetings of the European Council of Ministers, the Prime Minister and cabinet ministers all need to be clear with one another regarding the 'UK/EU' line they will be negotiating on once they are at the meeting. Other than the Prime Minister, it is the Chancellor of the Exchequer who will find himself or herself most likely to be called upon to exercise these crucial diplomatic political skills.

Membership of the European Union has given the United Kingdom executive an added dimension to its role that was obviously not an issue prior to joining. Membership of the EU has often been a crucial issue in respect to the doctrines of collective and individual ministerial responsibility. In 1975 Harold Wilson took the decision to free his cabinet ministers from collective responsibility so that they could campaign for either a 'no' or 'yes' vote in the referendum on continued membership of the European Union. European elections would provide another opportunity to set aside collective responsibility in 1977 while the issue of Europe proved to be the major obstacle to Cabinet unity for John Major during his term in office after the 1991 general election.

Membership of the European Union has also established a clear distinction between European law and United Kingdom law. Should there be any conflict between the provisions of European law and those of United Kingdom law, then it is European law that must prevail. As a signatory to the 1957 Treaty of Rome, the United Kingdom agrees that cases which reach the highest domestic court of appeal (in the United Kingdom this is the House of Lords), must be referred to the European Court of Justice (ECJ) in Luxembourg for a final hearing.

This European dimension to the work of the executive is a major aspect of its role. Lower courts in member states may ask the ECJ for rulings on the interpretation and meaning of treaties, while there is no appeal against decisions made by the ECJ. These powers, already substantial, have been extended by the Maastricht Treaty (1993) which gives the Court powers to fine member states for failing to comply with judgments.

Membership of the European Union has therefore required the development of a complex relationship between the executive and the courts in the United Kingdom. When courts have ruled that British law conflicts with European law, then the executive in the United Kingdom has been required to introduce new legislation that brings UK law into line with EU law. The executive therefore faces domestic courts with substantially more power than was the case before British membership of the European Union. The key case in establishing this dominance was the **Factortame Case** (1991). Factortame was an important case involving the registration of Spanish fishing vessels in Britain and a piece of UK legislation intended to prevent this. When examined through the facts of Factortame, the position of domestic courts and the ECJ becomes at once clearer, while bringing with it at the same time some crucial questions on the very nature of Parliamentary sovereignty.

A further consequence for the executive of UK membership of the EU has been the gradual pressure that has been applied to the notion of a unitary state. The regional emphasis on subnational government has resulted in EU funds flowing into regions independently of the executive and, since 1997, the creation of devolved assemblies in Scotland, Ireland and Wales.

In July 2005 the United Kingdom assumed the revolving presidency of the European Union for a six-month period. The opportunity to hold the presidency at this particular point could not have come at a more crucial time in the history of the Union. In May 2005, the French and Dutch electorates had delivered 'no' votes in referendums on the EU constitution and, as a consequence, tension between Britain and France heightened. During the presidency the Britain government will host a series of events under the general heading

Better Regulation Executive (BRE) that will seek to improve the dealings and delivery of EU business. Cabinet Office work during the UK presidency will also be co-ordinated by the Better Regulation Executive. In turn, the BRE will be supported by a **Better Regulation Task Force**, an independent body which advises government on action to ensure that regulation and enforcement of regulation meet the required standards. In June 2005, there were also two cabinet committees with specific European briefs although a closer look at the forty-plus committees and subcommittees reveals a much greaten impact by Europe and of EU issues on the whole structure of the cabinet committee system.

In short, continued British membership of the European Union continues to be a key factor in the nature of the relationship, not just between the executive and the legislature, but also between the executive and every other part of the system of government.

Concluding points

Chapter 1 has provided an introductory overview of the British executive: the central concern of this book. Having established the essential elements of our discussion, we may now move on to discuss each of them in more detail. In doing so, we are constructing an analysis of the British executive as it stands in the early years of the twenty-first century. We are concerned to discover how much power it has and where that power comes from. We are also concerned to understand more about the key players and institutions within the executive and how these players and institutions act and react within and around the internal and external mechanisms that seek to control them.

In putting together the various discussions in this book, and in outlining a wide range of theories and debates along the way, we shall be making a case that the British executive is not as all-powerful as some commentators have suggested. In discussing the Cabinet and the Prime Minister, it will become clear that, in many respects, the central executive does, indeed, have substantial powers and that, on occasion, these powers appear to override the scrutiny and control of Parliament. It will also be shown, however, that there is a significant number of factors that combine to control and constrain the executive and that leave the Prime Minister some distance removed from the type of 'President' that some observers claim to detect.

This is not to say that we will attempt to play down the power of the Prime Minister. The Prime Minister is clearly the most powerful figure in British politics and has a relationship with the Cabinet that has changed substantially in the later part of the post-war period. The changing nature of this relationship has done much to shift views that were once based around the traditional and historical understanding of what 'cabinet government' was supposed to represent. As we shall see, it is increasingly the case that the 'powers' and 'strengths' of the Prime Minister are, for better or worse, now linked inextricably to the leadership style and personality of the person in power. This, coupled with the Cabinet he or she appoints, and the methods by which he or she chooses to manage that Cabinet, reveal much about the nature and workings of the modern executive.

What you should have learnt from reading this chapter

You began this chapter by looking at some broad definitions of the executive. You should recall that our aim was to provide a basic overview of the British executive in its broadest sense that would give us a foundation on which to construct a detailed analysis of the Prime Minister and the Cabinet.

In giving a broad definition of the executive, we also defined the Cabinet and the Prime Minister, putting both of them briefly in their historical context and developing our understanding by making a clear distinction between the terms 'head of state' and 'head of government'. To emphasise these definitions further we also looked at a brief comparison of parliamentary and presidential systems.

We have also looked at the executive in terms of its relationship with the legislature. This was achieved in three key areas: Cabinet and Parliament, the Prime Minister and Parliament and the executive and the European Union.

The chapter concluded with a brief overview of the nature of the debates surrounding the executive, and made the case that the book will not necessarily be arguing the line that the British executive is over-powerful and out of control. Subsequent chapters in the book will show how Prime Minister and Cabinet remain constrained by a series of factors exercised mainly by the larger political system of the United Kingdom, along with some key external factors.

🔎 Glossary of key terms

Cabinet The leading members of the government, chosen by the Prime Minister to lead the department of a particular policy area. Traditionally the place where major government decisions are made.

Cabinet committees Appointed by the Prime Minister to deal with items of government business. Discussions in committee are supposed to inform decisions in full Cabinet. In June 2005, including subcommittees, there were around forty-two cabinet committees.

Cabinet Office Prepares the agendas and minutes of the Cabinet. Plays an important role in co-ordinating the work of government.

Collective cabinet responsibility The doctrine stating that all members of the government are collectively responsible for its decisions. In recent years it has been suggested that the application of the doctrine has undergone considerable change.

European Commission The permanent bureaucracy of the European Union. The primary role of the Commission is to initiate new European legislation.

European Council of Ministers The ultimate decision-making body of the European Union.

European Court of Justice The Court sits in Luxembourg and interprets European law. The decisions it makes are binding on all member states.

Executive The government – the body within a political system that runs the state.

Factortame Case (1991) An important case involving Spanish fishing fleets in British waters. The case established that in areas of EU legislative competence, EU law is supreme and the British courts must give it precedence over national UK law where the two conflict.

Glorious Revolution (1688) The culmination of the struggle between James II and William of Orange. Introduced a limited and constitutional monarchy upheld by a bill of rights which set out the rights of Parliament in relation to the monarch. Not to be confused with the US Bill of Rights that sets out the nature of the relationship between citizens and the state.

Government The elected individuals who make up the executive.

Head of government In the United Kingdom the Prime Minister.

Head of state The person who represents all the people of the state. In the United Kingdom, sometimes it's the Queen; on other occasions it's the Prime Minister. This situation has arisen because of the prerogative powers of the Prime Minister.

Individual ministerial responsibility Ministers are responsible to Parliament for their conduct as ministers and for the general work of their departments and the actions of their civil servants. Similar to collective cabinet responsibility in that observers question how effective the doctrine is in modern government.

Legislature The body in a political system that makes and/or passes laws. In the United Kingdom this function is performed by Parliament.

Parliamentary government The UK system whereby the legislature consists of two houses, the Commons and the Lords and where the Commons consists of members elected at least once every five years by people living in constituencies.

Prerogative powers The main source of the formal powers of the Prime Minister and derived from those once held by the monarch. Prerogative powers fall into two categories: those performed on behalf of the monarch as head of state and those performed as head of government.

Prime Minister The head of the British government. Since 1997 until the time of writing, this position has been held by Tony Blair.

Separation of powers The doctrine that requires the various institutions of the state to share the functions of government.

Uncodified Usually used to refer to the unwritten or 'uncodified' British Constitution as opposed to the written American Constitution. Large parts of the British Constitution are in fact written down, they're just not all together at the same time and place in the same document – hence they are 'uncodified'.

? Likely examination questions

Short questions

Describe what is meant by the term 'executive'.

Use your own words to produce short paragraph definitions for: Cabinet, Prime Minister, head of state, head of government.

Briefly describe the similarities and differences between parliamentary and presidential systems of government.

Describe what is meant by the term 'legislature'.

Briefly describe the nature of the relationship between the legislature and the executive.

Explain the significance of the Factortame Case (1991) for the UK executive.

Essay questions

To what extent does the UK executive illustrate the doctrine of separation of powers?

'The power of the UK legislature is compromised by membership of the EU.' Discuss.

Revision task

Use one side of one sheet of A3 paper to produce a revision diagram that shows all the following:

The structure of the UK executive branch of government.

The links between the UK executive and legislature.

The more terms from the Glossary (see above) that appear on your revision chart the greater its revision value to you.

Helpful websites

The British government has a large number of websites that will be useful to students of government and politics. These, and others listed here, are well worth a visit. Some government websites do appear to change domain from time to time. A good search engine such as 'Google' or 'Yahoo' will normally get you to where you want to be if any of the links here are no longer valid.

www.number10.gov.uk/

The 10 Downing Street website.

www.direct.gov.uk/

Particularly useful for department and Civil Service links.

www.cabinetoffice.gov.uk/

Very good for detailed studies of the central government machinery.

www.civilservice.gov.uk

As you would expect from the Civil Service, lots of material on structures and procedures but particularly good for tracking the often bewildering number of reforms to government bureaucracy.

www.parliament.uk

A very 'traditional' website and not always that easy to navigate. The search facility can be frustrating.

www.eu.org

For all things European.

http://news.bbc.co.uk/

An excellent website with very good search and archive facilities.

www.politicsassociation.com

The Politics Association was founded in 1969 to promote the teaching of politics. Their quickly developing website offers good links and lists of learning and teaching resources.

Suggestions for further reading

More detailed suggestions for further reading will be found at the end of the remaining chapters. For this overview of the central executive territory the following general texts will be useful starting points.

Coxall, B., Robins, L. and Leach, R. (2003) *Contemporary British Politics* 4th edn (Palgrave).

Dearlove, J. and Saunders, P. (2000) *Introduction to British Politics* (Polity Press).

Heywood, A. (1994) *Political Ideas and Concepts* (Macmillan).

Jones, B. and Kavanagh, D. (1998) *British Politics Today*, 6th edn (Manchester University Press).

Jones, B. (ed.) (2004) *Politics UK*, 5th edn (Longman Pearson).

Kingdom, J. (1999) *Government and Politics in Britain* (Polity Press).

McNaughton, N. (1999) *The Prime Minister and Cabinet Government* (Hodder).

McNaughton, N. (2001) *Success in Politics*, 2nd edn (Murray).

Moran, M. (2005) *Politics and Governance in the UK* (Palgrave).

Sampson, A. (2004) *Who Runs This Place? The Anatomy of Britain in the 21st Century* (Murray).

Wilson, C. (2003) *Understanding AS Level Government and Politics* (Manchester University Press).

CHAPTER 2

The Cabinet: Origins, Role and Structure

Contents

Overview

In the second chapter, we examine a broad range of issues relating to the origins and history, role and functions, and size and structure of the modern British system of cabinet government. By understanding the origins and basic functions of the Cabinet we will be better placed to discuss in detail the support system and bureaucracy of the Cabinet before going on to examine the various competing theories as to the future of the system of cabinet government as a whole.

Key issues to be covered in this chapter

- The development of the modern Cabinet
- The traditional and constitutional roles of the modern Cabinet
- An overview of the key functions of modern cabinets
- The size and structure of cabinets and the notion of cabinet hierarchies
- The selection and reshuffling of cabinets

Origins and history

The Glorious Revolution of 1688 is a useful starting point. This 'revolution' and subsequent settlement of 1689 provided a major turning point in the evolution of the British political system. Before 1688 the monarch reigned supreme. Parliament, if and when it was consulted, did little more than provide authority or legitimacy to the decisions taken by the monarch. In effect, the monarch could rule without Parliament for most of the time. The support of Parliament increased and consolidated the monarch's power, but it was not a prerequisite.

'Neither glorious nor a revolution' is a phrase frequently used to describe the events of 1688. In 1660, following the English Civil War and brief republic of Oliver Cromwell, the Stuart dynasty was restored but was, in the words of one writer, 'too stupid and arrogant' to accept the principle of constitutional monarchy. By the time James II had acceded to the throne in 1685 the Protestant nobility and gentry of England were rising against the centralising ambitions of the Roman Catholic monarch. Events came to a head in 1688 when the English nobility invited William III, the anti-French ruler of the Netherlands, to take over the throne. William agreed and went on to defeat James II in battle. The ensuing settlement – the 'Glorious Revolution' – established the dependence of the King on the support of Parliament and gave Parliament a veto over money matters. These events signify a major shift in the balance of political power away from the monarch and towards Parliament.

The phrase 'Cabinet' had been in use before 1688 to describe the small and élite group of advisers who clustered, court-like, around the monarch. After 1688 this group of people was required by William III to rule England. William needed to consolidate his power and run his new kingdom. He also found himself involved in a series of wars against France which required him to have the support of the majority in Parliament – the Whigs – who worked closely with William in deciding which policies and proposals would be acceptable to Parliament. The Cabinet therefore played a crucial role in this two-way communication between the Throne and Parliament. Essentially, the Cabinet had become 'semi-formalised'. It had none of the set procedures or party structures that we would recognise today and remained a loose set of arrangements until the following century.

A more recognisable version of the modern Cabinet evolved relatively quickly during the reign of George I. George was an uninterested and almost 'accidental' ruler of England who had no interest in the politics of his country and spoke little English. Under George I, the Cabinet, not the King, began to rule the country. When George did attend, he understood little and contributed even less. He very soon began to miss meetings and the Cabinet conducted business without him. George II was similarly disinterested in the day-to-day politics of running the country of which he was king, and it was not until George III that the monarch attempted to regain control of the system. George III reigned for a long time – 1760 to 1820 – and, unlike his predecessors, he did not consider himself to be a German first and King of England second.

Although not the first 'Prime Minister' in the way we would understand it – this accolade may be saved for Sir Robert Walpole – George III acted in a way that we would now associate with the Prime Minister. He attended meetings, he led the discussions and played a key role in the outcome of Cabinet deliberations. It was only the periods of insanity, which blighted George's life and became permanent after 1811, that required the senior ministers in the government to take over his roles.

The parliamentary reforms of the nineteenth century proved to be key accelerators in the development of what we now refer to as cabinet government. **Reform Acts** in 1832, 1867 and 1884/5 established a much larger electorate and encouraged the development of modern political parties. Voting discipline, party representation and constituency elections became central features of the House of Commons that became, after 1832, the stronger partner in the Commons/Lords relationship. Cabinet members were now drawn more from the Commons than the Lords as the influence of the monarch declined. As the role of the Cabinet developed alongside the changes listed above – especially the evolution of political parties – it became increasingly the case that the Cabinet was formed from the ranks of one political party and that the leadership of the party controlled cabinet membership. The monarch no longer decided who would sit in the Cabinet.

Role and functions of the modern Cabinet

While the basic roles and functions of the Cabinet are very similar to those that existed at the outset of the system, it is nevertheless important to recognise that there have been obvious changes to the traditional and constitutional roles.

Traditional and constitutional roles of the Cabinet

The Cabinet is the key committee in the executive. It consists usually of between twenty and twenty-five members drawn mainly from the largest party in the House of Commons.

The modern Cabinet has evolved from a number of traditional and constitutional roles. Initially, the Cabinet was the body in the executive where the key decisions of government were made. By the early eighteenth century the membership of the Cabinet was drawn from the House of Commons and the House of Lords, and consisted of a Prime Minister and leading ministers of the day. This key body dominated the legislature and the business of Parliament. The notion of collective cabinet responsibility may be traced back to these early days when it was acknowledged that the Cabinet should agree on policy in public, support the proposals and policies of the government in public and, in the event of the government being defeated in Parliament, then the Cabinet (and therefore the government) would resign. As Lord Melbourne said to his Cabinet in 1841, on the issue of the Corn Laws: 'Bye the bye, there is one thing we haven't agreed upon, which is, what are we to say? Is it better to make our corn dearer or cheaper, or to make the price steady? I don't care which: but we had better all tell the same story.'

The extent to which collective decision-making continues to exist in its traditional form will be the focus of a much more detailed discussion in the following chapter. In terms of key functions of the Cabinet, the following list provides a fairly comprehensive overview of exactly what role the Cabinet plays in modern British government. When reading this list, it is worth keeping in mind the notion of 'traditional', as opposed to modern, roles, and being prepared to question the extent to which some of the functions that appear here continue to reflect the reality of the modern Cabinet. Cabinet:

- Makes the final 'decision' on policy to be submitted to Parliament. Although it no longer actually decides many policies in terms of the detail, it remains the place at which the most important decisions are registered. It would be more accurate, therefore, to see this particular role as giving formal approval to decisions taken elsewhere.
- Gives legitimacy and authority to government decisions.
- Develops a common government message for the media and for Parliament.
- Has supreme control over the national executive.
- Provides co-ordination and delimitation of the departments of state.
- Plans the business of Parliament.
- Provides political leadership for the party, in Parliament and for the country.
- Arbitrates in cases of disputes between departments. In recent years prime ministers have appointed 'enforcers' to carry out this function.
- Provides crisis management during emergencies and on issues likely to result in major political controversy.

You will see from this list that the Cabinet has what is essentially a dual role – it proposes legislation and it then supervises the administration of that legislation. The list can give only a snapshot of the complex web of functions and roles of the Cabinet, however. The reasons for this difficulty in defining exactly what the Cabinet does should by now be familiar. First, the uncodified British Constitution gives no clear role to the Cabinet, and second, every Cabinet is to a large extent a creation of the Prime Minister of the day and, as such, a reflection of how that person wishes to organise the running of government.

The changing role of the modern Cabinet
Given the flexible nature of the British constitutional arrangements and the personalised nature of cabinet management, it is fairly obvious that the institution will have changed considerably over the years. As we have already explained, the impact of a century of political reform in the 1800s and the huge growth of government

following World War II have drastically changed the character and nature of cabinet government. Alongside the physical expansion of government, Cabinet has also had to adapt to the increasingly complex and detailed workings of government departments, especially the way in which the workings of these departments have become ever closer and more interlinked. When one considers this alongside the huge growth in bureaucracy, administration and support that has accompanied the growth of government, it becomes clear that the Cabinet itself would obviously have changed over the same period.

Is cabinet government alive and well? This is certainly something we shall discuss in more detail in Chapter 3, but it should by now be apparent why the question is raised at all. With a huge and ever-growing workload, an expanded network of cabinet committees, and the arrival of increasing numbers of outside specialists and personal advisers, it is little wonder that some critics worry that Cabinet is losing full control over the government's policies and decisions. Under these circumstances and with ongoing changes, it is 'inevitable', in the words of a number of commentators, that the traditional role of Cabinet has been 'eroded'. As we shall discuss at length elsewhere, however, this rather gloomy view of the modern Cabinet may be overcritical and based on a meaningless comparison with cabinets from as far back as the nineteenth century. We shall certainly want to examine the argument that what we have in the United Kingdom now is less a Cabinet that would have been recognised by Melbourne and Salisbury and more a modern 'system' of Cabinet that better reflects the nature of twenty-first-century politics while maintaining the underlying principles of what cabinet government should be. It's certainly different, but it's not dead yet.

Size and structure

While the number of government members may be over 100, the membership of the Cabinet is usually somewhere between twenty and twenty-five. The size of the British Cabinet is significant and will be discussed in the 'Small v. Big' part of this chapter. The terms 'Cabinet' and 'government' are no longer synonymous. The modern Cabinet represents only a very small part of what has become a very complex structure of government that forms, as we shall go on to see,

Table 2.1 The Cabinet (June 2005)

Prime Minister, First Lord of the Treasury and Minister for the Civil Service	Rt Hon. Tony Blair MP
Deputy Prime Minister and First Secretary of State	Rt Hon. John Prescott MP
Chancellor of the Exchequer	Rt Hon. Gordon Brown MP
Secretary of State for Foreign and Commonwealth Affairs	Rt Hon. Jack Straw MP
Secretary of State for Environment, Food and Rural Affairs	Rt Hon. Margaret Beckett MP
Secretary of State for Transport and Secretary of State for Scotland	Rt Hon. Alistair Darling MP
Secretary of State for Health	Rt Hon. Patricia Hewitt MP
Chancellor of the Duchy of Lancaster (Minister for the Cabinet Office)	Rt Hon. John Hutton MP
Secretary of State for Northern Ireland and Secretary of State for Wales	Rt Hon. Peter Hain MP
Secretary of State for Defence	Rt Hon. John Reid MP
Secretary of State for Trade and Industry	Rt Hon. Alan Johnson MP
Secretary of State for Culture, Media and Sport	Rt Hon. Tessa Jowell MP
Parliamentary Secretary to the Treasury (Chief Whip)	Rt Hon. Hilary Armstrong MP
Secretary of State for the Home Department	Rt Hon. Charles Clarke MP
Chief Secretary to the Treasury	Rt Hon. Des Browne MP
Leader of the House of Commons, Lord Privy Seal	Rt Hon. Geoffrey Hoon MP
Minister without Portfolio and Party Chair	Rt Hon. Ian McCartney MP
Leader of the House of Lords and Lord President of the Council	Rt Hon. Baroness Amos
Secretary of State for Constitutional Affairs and Lord Chancellor	Rt Hon. Lord Falconer of Thoroton
Secretary of State for International Development	Rt Hon. Hilary Benn MP
Secretary of State for Work and Pensions	Rt Hon. David Blunkett MP
Secretary of State for Education and Skills	Rt Hon. Ruth Kelly MP

Table 2.1 (continued)

Minister of Communities and Local Government	Rt Hon. David Miliband MP
Also attend Cabinet meetings:	
Attorney General	Rt Hon. Lord Goldsmith
Minister of State for Europe	Mr Douglas Alexander MP
Lords Chief Whip	Lord Grocott

a clear hierarchy of individuals that rises up from the lowly junior parliamentary secretaries to those promoted to be full cabinet ministers. The list here shows the Cabinet as it was formed after the 2005 general election.

We have already explained that most cabinet members are drawn from the House of Commons but it is also the case that some cabinet members may sit in the House of Lords. You will remember that the Lord Chancellor (also referred to now as the Secretary of State for Constitutional Affairs) is a member of the House of Lords who holds a cabinet position. Most members of the Cabinet will be ministers in charge of Whitehall departments. The person appointed to be Chancellor of the Duchy of Lancaster is in a slightly different situation in that the duties of this position are located in the Cabinet Office and range over a broad spread of policy issues that cut across departmental responsibilities and often include the 'referee' role in disputes between departments and their ministers.

Cabinet hierarchy

Depending on which metaphor you choose to use, the Cabinet sits either at the apex or core of either the hierarchy or web of government. While it is clear that the Cabinet enjoys this position relative to the rest of government, it is also important to point out that the Cabinet itself reflects an inner hierarchy.

The most senior members of the Cabinet are usually considered to be:

- The Prime Minister
- The Chancellor of the Exchequer

- The Foreign Secretary
- The Home Secretary

In recent years it has been possible to add the office of the **Deputy Prime Minister** who is also the First Secretary of State to this list.

These positions are widely acknowledged to be the 'great' offices of state, and it has more often than not been the case that a prime minister will have occupied one or more of these positions prior to becoming the First Lord of the Treasury. The two most controversial and studied of modern prime ministers have bucked this particular trend, however. The following table illustrates this point:

Nevertheless, the clear sense of hierarchy in the Cabinet remains. If we move away from the key offices of state discussed above, we encounter the secretaries of state for the big-spending departments, such as Health, Defence and Education, through to the less politically significant, and therefore less politically powerful, departments, such as Culture, Media and Sport. Moving further down the ladder we meet those junior ministers with portfolios (or responsibilities) for only a part of the work of a department and who will not attend cabinet meetings. It will also be seen from the list of cabinet ministers (above) that one person – the Minister for Europe – attends cabinet meetings even though there is no 'Department for Europe', and that the Attorney General and the Chief Whip in the House of Lords also attend the gatherings of this inner circle of government. It should also be noted that, in the case of Communities and Local Government, there is no separate Whitehall department. This particular aspect of government is included in the broad remit of the Office of the Deputy of Prime Minister along with a whole host of 'social' issues such as homelessness, housing, planning, regions, science and

Table 2.2 Before he/she was Prime Minister

Tony Blair: PM 1997–	No government experience
John Major: PM 1990–2, 1992–7	1989 – Foreign Secretary
	1990 – Chancellor of the Exchequer
Margaret Thatcher: PM 1979–90	1974 – Brief period at Education

research, social exclusion and urban policy. Single government departments have in recent times covered many of these areas. This makes the Office of the Deputy Prime Minister a powerful yet frequently overlooked and underestimated part of government.

Cabinet size: small v. big

The average size of the modern British Cabinet is twenty. For most of World War II, Winston Churchill managed a Cabinet of between five and eight members. Leaving aside Churchill's less than successful experiment of 1951 (see below) and other wartime arrangements, peacetime cabinets in the United Kingdom have ranged from sixteen under Andrew Bonar-Law in 1922 to twenty-four under Harold Wilson in 1964 and the twenty-six of the Blair 2005 administration.

There are four key factors that explain the growth of the size of British Cabinets.

- **The growth of the state and the public sector** is probably the most important and significant reason. From the social reforms of Gladstone and Disraeli through to the Liberal reforms before World War I and on to the creation of the Welfare State after 1945, the state has grown massively and government has taken on more and more areas of responsibility. It is now the case that most aspects of modern life and society are in some way covered by government departments and therefore by cabinet ministers. Even where change has occurred (the disappearance of the Ministry of Agriculture, for instance) it is more likely to be the case that areas will simply resurface under a new name, new organisation. In the case of agriculture, we now have the department of Environment, Food and Rural Affairs. Compare the May 2005 Cabinet with the first Blair administration of 1997 and you will see other long-gone departments such as Social Security and Environment that have merged with, or been gobbled up by, other areas of government. The size of the Cabinet, however, has grown from twenty-two 'full' members in 1997 to the twenty-six of 2005.

- **The proliferation of interest groups and pressure from these groups** may be seen as a second reason for the growth in size of the Cabinet. Groups outside Westminster have pressurised government over the years to the point where many sectors that were previously unrepresented in the Cabinet, such as education, health, culture and local government, are now present around the cabinet table in the shape of a secretary of state or represented within a department by a junior minister. Another example of this type of pressure may be detected in the pressure from Scottish, Welsh and some Irish interests to have full recognition in Cabinet and, more recently, to use those positions to push for devolution.

- **The higher levels of the civil service** provide a third reason for the growth of the numbers in Cabinet. Career civil servants see cabinet representation as the clearest sign of the political significance of their particular area and are reluctant to take part in any process that would genuinely slim government down at this particular level.
- **The increase in prime ministerial patronage** is the fourth and final key reason for the growth in size of the British Cabinet. The larger the Cabinet, then the more opportunities a Prime Minister has to manage the factions in his or her party be it in the form of rewarding loyalty and talent, balancing the 'court' of rivals, acknowledging party 'favourites' or keeping loose cannons as close as possible.

Observers inside and outside the cabinet system have tended to criticise the larger cabinets much more than the smaller ones. The World War I cabinets of Lloyd George and the already noted World War II cabinets of Winston Churchill are largely considered to have been more effective than the larger versions. War tends to be the main force behind moves towards smaller cabinets. Alongside those already mentioned, it is worth noting that Blair, Major and Thatcher all experimented at some point with smaller cabinets during the Kosovo, Gulf and Falklands wars.

Criticisms of larger cabinets tend to focus on a wide-ranging list of shortcomings that include:

- The cabinet process becomes too slow.
- Decision making in the Cabinet becomes cumbersome and difficult.

- Factions and competing political and departmental interests around the cabinet table hamper clear decision making.
- Too many members make it difficult to maintain meaningful collective responsibility.
- Large cabinets lack the necessary strategic vision.
- Ministers get locked into complicated struggles for resources with lots of other ministers and see no further than departmental interests.

Discussions on the relative merits of small as opposed to large cabinets are important. The debate is about the constitutional role of what the Cabinet is supposed to be and do, not purely about the technical details of departments, responsibilities, and the relationship between civil servants and ministers. Denis Kavanagh neatly sums up the dilemma surrounding ideal cabinet size:

> Decisions about Cabinet size and composition have to balance the needs of decision making and deliberation against those of representativeness. It has to be small enough to allow ministers the opportunities to discuss, deliberate and coordinate major policies, yet it must also be large enough to include heads of major departments and accommodate different political views in the party.[1]

Prime ministers have, on and off, expressed the wish to experiment with smaller cabinets. Leo Amery, a cabinet member in the Bonar Law and Baldwin administrations, argued that government would be much more effective through a 'Policy Cabinet' of around six or seven members who would have no departmental ties and who would be able to bring an overarching and strategic perspective to the full range of policy concerns, not just the vested interests of individual department briefs. In 1951 Winston Churchill experimented with a Cabinet of sixteen that included three 'overlords' – ministers who sat in the House of Lords, free from constituency or departmental duties, and who had the responsibility for the co-ordination of policies in related departments. This was a major political experiment and a major failure. The 'normal' structure of the Cabinet was back in place after less than two years when it became clear that it was very difficult to separate the co-ordinating responsibilities of the three 'overlords' in the upper chamber from the duties of ministers formally answerable to the Commons. As Kavanagh has commented: 'it is easier to separate policy from administration in theory than it is in practice'.[2]

In recent years the concept of the 'inner cabinet' has been discussed in relation to the debate on the relative merits of size. The phrase 'inner Cabinet' is often used interchangeably with 'kitchen Cabinet' even though the two have considerable differences.

'Inner cabinets' tend to be very much political creations that exist just beneath the outer veneer of the Cabinet and consist of four or five key ministers closest to the Prime Minister who meet independently of the full Cabinet. The Labour cabinet minister Richard Crossman, who claimed that during the Wilson government he had been a member of such a group, first described the existence of these inner cabinets in the 1960s. Patrick Gordon Walker, who served in the Cabinet under both Attlee and Wilson, used the phrase 'partial cabinets' to describe what was essentially the same phenomenon: frequent meetings, designed to suit Downing Street, that take place between departmental ministers and the Prime Minister in such a way as to leave out ministers who have no responsibility for action. According to Richard Rose, these 'partial cabinets' now have their formal expression in many cabinet committees.[3] Nevertheless, the existence of inner cabinets is seen by some observers to be a threat to the nature of genuine collective cabinet government. Other commentators have balanced this view, however, by making a more pragmatic and realistic case for what is in essence the informal evolution of 'policy cabinets' of the kind that Churchill experimented with in the early 1950s.

The existence and functioning of these inner 'policy cabinets' remains, for some people at least, an unresolved problem of the successful separation of policy and administration of the kind alluded to earlier by Kavanagh. In his 1984 Reith Lectures, the ex-joint head of the Civil Service, Douglas Wass, questioned the principle that strategic policy making could be separated from day-to-day procedural matters by making the point that he found it virtually impossible to think constructively about general policy issues without the opportunity beforehand to have been involved in particular practical cases. These meetings can often include individuals from outside the Cabinet, such as key back-benchers, certain key public officials or leading public figures, and may even include private citizens.

Kitchen cabinets tend to differ from inner cabinets in that those who become 'members' of this type of group are drawn from a much wider and personal group of prime ministerial confidants than the mostly political grouping that characterises the inner Cabinet. The phrase was first used to describe the small group of individuals surrounding Harold Wilson as his closest political advisers. Marcia Williams (later Lady Falkender), who was Wilson's Political Secretary, and Joe Haines, his Press Officer, were the key 'members' of this kitchen Cabinet who may, on the face of it, have held fairly lowly positions, yet wielded enormous influence on Wilson himself. If the Cabinet occupies some vague aspect of the Constitution in a darkened corner of the sitting room, and if the inner Cabinet lurks somewhere at the back of the dining room, then the kitchen Cabinet really is hidden away somewhere in a makeshift constitutional loft as a kind of lagging on the prime ministerial pipes: completely unofficial, wholly unaccountable, yet almost indispensable.

The kitchen Cabinet offers the Prime Minister an informal support network. Margaret Thatcher's kitchen cabinets were largely reckoned to be based around her private office and almost certainly included her foreign affairs adviser, Charles Powell, a civil servant transferred to her private office (and probably responsible for encouraging her to push forward a strategy that distanced the United Kingdom from the European Union), her Press Secretary, Bernard Ingham, and in the later years her Parliamentary Private Secretary, Ian Gow.

In common with his recent predecessors, Tony Blair has formed around himself a kitchen Cabinet through which a small number of select and trusted advisers and friends have passed since the general election victory in 1997. In those early years people like Alastair Campbell (Press Secretary until 2001), Jonathon Powell (Chief of Staff), Nick Brown (Chief Whip) and David Milliband (Head of the Policy Unit) combined with senior cabinet ministers, such as Gordon Brown, Robin Cook, Ann Taylor and John Prescott, to form a close-knit circle of advisers. The role of Peter Mandelson is particularly interesting. In an eventful political career that has seen him play a key role in the 'project' of modernising the Labour Party, manage the 1997 election victory, take an early role in government of 'co-ordinating policy', resign twice and then be appointed Commissioner for Trade in the European Union, Mandelson may well be, along with Cherie Blair, one of the constant sources of advice and support to the Prime Minister, either in or out of whatever 'structure' the kitchen Cabinet may currently have.

'Inner' or 'kitchen' – the criticism remains that a system which allows both these unofficial 'policy' or 'partial' cabinets to coalesce around a Prime Minister who already dominates an unwieldy and overlarge Cabinet is hardly likely to be beneficial to the health of effective and efficient collective government. As we shall see in Chapter 3, however, when we discuss the current debate on collective cabinet government, and again in Chapter 8, where we discuss the concept of the core executive, it will become fairly clear that the size of the modern Cabinet is not the only problem that some commentators choose to highlight in the workings of the central committee of the British executive.

Cabinet ministers: how to be appointed

In 1989, from a background in banking and Lambeth Council, followed by ten years in the House of Commons as the Conservative MP for Huntingdon, Margaret Thatcher appointed John Major Foreign Secretary. Major's stay at the Foreign Office was brief. In less than a year he had been moved to the Treasury as Chancellor of the Exchequer where his tenure was as brief as his stay in the Foreign Office. In 1991 he was elected leader of the Conservative Party after the fall of Thatcher and thus became the Prime Minister of the United Kingdom. The qualifications for particular ministerial posts are not always obvious.

The political journey of John Major is not the only example we could use of the seemingly random and *ad hoc* appointment and shuffling of ministers of the Crown. If we use the present government as an example, we are able to see that expertise in any given field of policy is frequently the least desirable quality in those called upon to serve.

If we look at the previous Conservative administrations then similar patterns occur. As well as the political odyssey of John Major, we could track the journey of Ken Clarke from Health in 1998, Education in 1990, Home Office in 1992 and finally to the Treasury as Chancellor in 1993. The movement of a Conservative minister in

Table 2.3 The movement of ministers

Robin Cook – Foreign Secretary in the first Blair government but had been moved to the position of President of the Council and Leader of the Commons by 2002. Resigned from government over the war in Iraq in March 2003. Died, August 2005.

David Blunkett – In 1997 Blunkett was in charge of Education and Employment. By 2003 he had been moved to the Home Office, a position from which he was forced to resign in 2004. He re-entered government in 2005 as Secretary of State for Work and Pensions.

Alistair Darling – Chief Secretary to the Treasury in 1997, Transport in 2002, Secretary of State for Transport *and* Secretary of State for Scotland in 2005.

John Reid – not in government in 1987. Minister without Portfolio and Party Chair in 2002, Health in 2004, Defence in 2005.

Charles Clarke – Education in 2002, Home Secretary 2005.

the 1980s from Agriculture to Education is a particularly good illustration of the random nature of British ministerial appointments: farmyards one day, classrooms the next. Clearly, expertise coupled with a deep and detailed knowledge of a given policy area are not the key factors in determining ministerial appointments. So how do ministers get themselves appointed?

It is worth noting that, while the number of cabinet positions has remained relatively stable for over 100 years, the number of appointments to government positions outside the Cabinet has risen substantially. Research has shown how Clement Attlee was able to hand out ninety-five government appointments in 1950. This figure had risen to 123 by the second year of the Thatcher period in 1980. The number of government appointments in 2005 is somewhere around the 130 mark. Most of these positions are non-cabinet ministers of state, junior ministers and the lowly parliamentary private secretaries in the House of Commons (who are, nevertheless, bound by the doctrine of collective cabinet responsibility.) This represents political patronage on a huge scale and is a major advantage to any Prime Minister. Those who benefit from this patronage will usually need to be able to place ticks against all or some of the following criteria for appointment:

- **Time served on the slippery pole** – in other words, most appointments (especially to the higher positions) will be of those people who have put in the appropriate amount of time ascending the ministerial hierarchy. These people will have begun their ministerial careers as PPSs (parliamentary private secretaries) and will have looked to progress through time spent as a junior minister then as a minister outside the Cabinet and then, they hope, a full Cabinet position. The new Chancellor of the Duchy of Lancaster (Minister for the Cabinet Office) is a good example of this. John Hutton entered Parliament in 1992 and, in 1998, was appointed PPSs to Margaret Beckett at the Board of Trade from where he followed her to her new position as Leader of the Commons in 1999. He presumably impressed those around him in this role and was soon 'shuffled' to the Department of Health where he rose through the ranks to become Minister of State for Health in 2001. Hutton was appointed as a full cabinet member as Minister for the Cabinet Office in May 2005. If, at any point in this journey Hutton had given the impression of 'not being up to the job', then he would have risen no higher (probably no higher than his position as PPS) and would have found himself on the back benches once again.

- **Time served in the House of Commons** – this is perhaps less important than was once the case. Research continues to show that the average time spent in the House of Commons before becoming a cabinet minister is fourteen years. The career of John Hutton, as outlined above, reflects this fairly accurately. There are examples, however, especially in the current government, of ministers with far less parliamentary experience. Ruth Kelly, the Secretary of State for Education did not enter the Commons until 1997, and David Milliband was made Minister for Communities and Local Government having only been elected in 2001. Time served in the Commons was once felt to be the necessary 'apprenticeship' for those who aspired to high office. The fact that this is not now necessary probably says more about the position of the Commons than it does about ministers in general.

- **Time served in opposition** – this is one factor that many of the more established members of the current government are able to lay claim to. Labour was in opposition from 1979 to 1997 and could field only one minister with past ministerial experience upon its return to power. Most cabinet members in a government returning to office after a period in opposition will have been members of the opposition 'Shadow' Cabinet where front-bench spokespeople will 'shadow' the government minister for their particular area. Membership of the Shadow Cabinet is therefore seen as a useful preparation for the 'real thing' once the party returns to power. Both of the main parties use the shadow system although the process is much more formalised in the Labour Party where the Shadow Cabinet is chosen by the National Executive Committee and where a Labour leader who has just become Prime Minister is required to choose his or her first Cabinet from this NEC-selected group.

- **Time served in the party** is probably another factor that is less important than it once was. It does improve the chances of an individual being appointed to the Cabinet, however. Current examples could include John Prescott's long tenure as the Deputy Prime Minister and Margaret Beckett's equally long career on the front bench. The relatively short-lived cabinet careers of Mo Mowlam and Clare Short are also examples of individuals who, while no doubt possessed of genuine political ability, could also look to their standing in the Labour Party as a factor in their elevation to the Cabinet.

- **A safe pair of hands** – 'steady', 'dependable', 'safe', just three of the adjectives used to describe a current member of the Cabinet by his constituency secretary during a conversation as part of the preparation of this book. It is certainly the case that those individuals with proven track records of effective department management will be regarded as good choices for one of the 'higher' cabinet positions.

- **The right faction** – those prospective ministers who have positioned themselves in or around the prime ministerial grouping may be more likely to be elevated to the Cabinet than those individuals who are more associated with the 'court' of a key rival. This type of 'court' politics is becoming an increasingly important factor in the current Cabinet composition and was particularly noticeable in the aftermath of the 2005 election when a handful of ministers appeared to be able to influence the decisions being made by a Prime Minister faced with a much-reduced majority in the House of Commons. It is also the case on occasions that the Prime Minister will appoint a political 'enemy' to the Cabinet in order to buy his or her silence and pacify a particular group or wing in the party.

Cabinet ministers: how to get sacked

Being removed from the Cabinet appears to be considerably easier than getting there in the first place. In both instances it is the Prime Minister who will make the decision and, for most people who leave the Cabinet (with one or two notable exceptions, as we shall see), it usually signifies the end of a political career at the highest level. Occasionally, ministers may resign from the Cabinet, often with spectacular political consequences and fall-out.

The Cabinet is regularly 'shuffled'. This involves the movement of individuals in and out of the system and also involves a brief burst of musical chairs around the coffin-shaped table of the Cabinet Room as ministers move from Defence to NATO (George Robertson, 2003) or from Education to the Home Office (Charles Clarke, December 2004).

There is a number of reasons for reshuffling a Cabinet. The Prime Minister may feel that a particular policy area is not performing well and would benefit from a new approach by some other person, or it might be felt that an individual minister is simply not up to the job – for a variety of reasons. In recent years Cabinet reshuffles have become part of larger restructurings of government departments. It is interesting to note that, although we have explained how the number of people in government is steadily rising, the actual number of departments is in decline. There were thirty departments in 1950, nineteen in 1993 and seventeen in 1997. Blair has been particularly active in this restructuring process. He has created the Department of the Environment, Food and Rural Affairs in place of the old Ministry of Agriculture, Fisheries and Food, and he has also created a new Department of International Development.

If we move on to look at the sacking of ministers, then a fairly clear set of criteria emerges. Public (and therefore high-profile) sackings are actually quite rare. Many ministers likely to be despatched by the Prime Minister engage in the traditional exchange of letters beforehand and usually resign. What follows is a list of the kind of behaviour that is almost guaranteed to leave a minister back on the back benches and/or spending more time with his or her family.

- **Failure to comply with the doctrine of collective cabinet responsibility** is the most obvious reason for a cabinet minister either to resign or be sacked. Recent examples already discussed elsewhere in this book include Michael Heseltine and his disagreement with the Cabinet over the sale of Westland Helicopters, – resignation and Clare Short and her somewhat protracted process of resignation over her opposition to the war in Iraq. Robin Cook resigned his position as Leader of the House for similar reasons. This is not to say, however, that transgressions of collective responsibility will always result in dismissal or resignation. The problems faced by Major in his Cabinet after 1992 were largely to do with attitudes to Europe and the lack of a collective Cabinet position. Several ministers, including Michael Portillo and John Redwood, were clearly briefing against the government and would ordinarily have been forced to resign or be sacked. Under these particular circumstances, Major felt it better to have them where he could see them as opposed to the greater set of problems of finding them completely free from all notion of collective responsibility.
- **Policy problems** of the kind experienced by Norman Lamont (Britain's crash out of the European Monetary System in 1993), and Edwina Currie (who in 1983 correctly claimed that most British egg production was contaminated with salmonella) are two examples of where cabinet ministers have been responsible for major policy disasters and have had no option but to resign rather than wait to be sacked. The current government has had a slightly better track record than most in this particular respect. Large-scale errors and policy disaster areas, such as the Millennium Dome, the foot-and-mouth outbreak and the 2005 problems with overpaid Family Tax Credits have required few ministerial sacrifices. It is noticeable that the conventions that govern minis-

terial sacking and resignations over policy issues have shifted somewhat. It is difficult to imagine a set of circumstances now similar to those that brought about the resignation of Sir Thomas Dugdale over the Crichel Down affair in 1954. Even the more recent resignation of Lord Carrington in 1982 because of his failure to heed warnings of an Argentinian invasion of the Falklands looks to be from some quaint and older age. The resignation of Stephen Byers in 2002 may look like a minister falling over major policy problems yet the affair was drawn out and lengthy and may have had more to do with pressure from Labour back-benchers than any particular crisis of honour for Byers himself. When we turn to our next category, however, we will find ourselves on much richer ground as far as the potential for sackings and resignations is concerned.

- **Personal problems** of either a financial or sexual sort have accounted for a large number of ministerial resignations in recent years. Cecil Parkinson (1985), David Mellor (1992), Tim Yeo (1994), Lord Caithness (1994), Robert Hughes (1995) and Ron Davies (1998) are all examples of ministerial resignations necessitated by events far away from the cabinet table and departments of state.
- **Issues of ministerial responsibility** tend to be those types of happening where the minister has acted in a way that is not entirely conducive to his or her role as a government minister and yet may not be entirely 'personal' as explained in the previous paragraph. Examples of this are to be found in Leon Brittan's resignation over leaking documents relating to the Westland affair, Tim Smith and Neil Hamilton's acceptance of 'cash for questions' in 1994, and David Willetts's secret direction of Conservative members of the Privileges Committee while still a government whip. Occasionally, these issues of ministerial responsibility merge murkily with the personal problems listed above. David Blunkett's fast tracking of a passport for the nanny of his married lover is a particularly good example from the present government.

Given the examples we have used here it should come as no surprise to realise that, in choosing and managing a Cabinet, the Prime Minister has a difficult job. Nor does the Prime Minister have an entirely free hand in the selection of those who will serve. For a start, all members of the Cabinet must be drawn from either the Commons or the Lords, and a Cabinet must always contain at least two peers, the Leader of the House of Lords and the Lord Chancellor. Having made that point, there have been in recent years examples of peers appointed to Cabinet with relatively short party political careers. Margaret Thatcher appointed Lord Young as Secretary of State for Employment between 1985 and 1987 and then as Secretary of State at the Department of Trade and Industry in 1987. Lord Cockfield had an even wider-ranging political career starting in the Department of Trade, moving to the Duchy of Lancaster, before ending up as a European commissioner. More recently, Tony Blair has created a number of life peerages for individuals and then given them ministerial posts. The most notable of these appointments is Lord Falconer, a lawyer friend of the Blairs, who now finds himself Secretary of State for Constitutional Affairs and Lord Chancellor.

Having looked in some detail into the role, functions and composition of modern cabinets, we can move on to Chapter 3 and examine the support systems of modern cabinet government – cabinet committees and the cabinet secretariat.

....

✓ **What you should have learnt from reading this chapter**

Chapter 2 has begun to add more detail to our knowledge of the structure, origins and role of the Cabinet. It should now be clear how the Cabinet evolved from the constitutional arrangements agreed around the time of the Glorious Revolution of 1688 and how the role of the monarchy in Cabinet was gradually altered during the political reforms of the nineteenth century.

We have also examined the changing nature of the Cabinet in British politics and have highlighted discussions on cabinet hierarchies and the relative merits of large as opposed to smaller cabinets. By looking in more detail at the composition of the Cabinet we have noted the various factors that determine how any individual might be promoted to the Cabinet, and we have also looked at those factors that will require a minister either to resign or be sacked. Our discussion of the Cabinet so far is revealing a very complex and complicated organism. We will move on to look at the internal structures in more depth in Chapter 3.

🔍 Glossary of key terms

Cabinet hierarchy The clearly defined hierarchy of posts within the Cabinet based on the Prime Minister, Chancellor, Foreign Secretary and Home Secretary. Hierarchies are often reflected in the membership of key cabinet committees or in the membership of 'inner' cabinets.

Deputy Prime Minister The role has no constitutional definition and the role varies according to the wishes of the Prime Minister. In recent years the position is often linked with attempts to co-ordinate the work of government.

Inner cabinets Smaller groups within the Cabinet that meet with the Prime Minister to discuss specific policy areas and issues.

Interest groups Pressure groups that represent the interests of particular economic or occupational groups, especially business organisations, professional associations and trade unions.

Kitchen cabinets Similar to inner cabinets but will involve the presence of people from outside the Cabinet.

Prime ministerial patronage The posts, promotions, resources and connections that the Prime Minister has the ability to give and remove from individuals or groups within or connected to government.

Reform Acts – 1832, 1867, 1884–5 The series of political reforms in the nineteenth century that gradually increased the size of the electorate and was therefore partly responsible for the growth of mass parties and increased the need for cabinet discipline.

? Likely examination questions

Short questions

Describe what is meant by the term 'Cabinet'.

Briefly describe the origins of the cabinet system of government.

Describe the role of the Prime Minister in relation to the rest of the Cabinet.

Describe the key functions of the Cabinet.

Briefly describe the criteria for a successful promotion to Cabinet.

Explain the reasons why cabinet ministers are almost always 'ex-cabinet' ministers at some point in their career.

Essay questions

Use examples you are familiar with to discuss the changing roles of the modern Cabinet.

To what extent would you agree with the suggestion that smaller cabinets function better than larger cabinets?

Revision task

Use this chapter to produce a two-sided leaflet explaining the role and functions of the Cabinet.

 Helpful websites

www.number10.gov.uk/

www.direct.gov.uk/

www.cabinetoffice.gov.uk/

www.civilservice.gov.uk

www.parliament.uk

 Suggestions for further reading

Burch, M. and Halliday, I. (1996) *The British Cabinet System* (Prentice Hall).

Coxall, B., Robins, L. and Leach, R. (2003) *Contemporary British Politics*, 4th edn (Palgrave), chapter 12.

Jones, B. (ed.) (2004) *Politics UK*, 5th edn (Longman Pearson), chapter 19.

Jones, B. and Kavanagh, D. (1998) *British Politics Today*, 6th edn (Manchester University Press).

Kavanagh, D. and Seldon, A. (1999) *The Powers behind the Prime Minister* (HarperCollins).

Kingdom, J. (1999) *Government and Politics in Britain* (Polity Press).

McNaughton, N. (1999) *The Prime Minister and Cabinet Government* (Hodder), chapter 2.

McNaughton, N. (2001) *Success in Politics*, 2nd edn (Murray), Unit 8.

Rose, R. (2001) *The Prime Minister in a Shrinking World* (Polity Press).

Sampson, A. (2004) *Who Runs This Place? The Anatomy of Britain in the 21st Century* (Murray), chapter 7.

Thomas, G. (1998) *Prime Minister and Cabinet Today* (Manchester University Press).

Thomas, G. (2002) 'The Prime Minister and Cabinet', *Politics Review*, vol. 11.4, 2002.

CHAPTER 3

The Cabinet: Support and Bureaucracy

Contents

Overview

In this third chapter, we continue to look at the workings of the Cabinet. Having looked in detail at the origins, structure and functions of the Cabinet, it is now necessary to analyse the structures around the Cabinet that allow the workings of cabinet government to continue in what is now a very complex and layered central government system. We will examine the organisation and functions of cabinet committees and will look in some detail at the Cabinet Office and the Cabinet Secretariat.

Key issues to be covered in this chapter

- The development of cabinet committees
- The use of cabinet committees by recent prime ministers
- The effectiveness of cabinet committees
- The structure and role of the Cabinet Office
- The structure and role of the Cabinet Secretariat
- The Cabinet Office and Secretariat under Tony Blair
- Recent reforms to the workings and structure of the Cabinet Office

Introduction

Modern cabinet government requires a substantial substructure and organisation for it to continue to fulfil its functions in accordance with what people feel is the 'proper' way for the system to work. The two main parts of the system that we shall discuss in this chapter are not particularly new innovations. **Cabinet committees** and the **Cabinet Office** may be traced back to the reforms introduced by David Lloyd George in order to re-structure a government in such a way that it would be more capable of co-ordinating what was, by 1916, war on a scale that had never before been witnessed by an industrial society. The debates and discussions that will be outlined in this chapter cut across several of the key themes in the book. The nature of the Prime Minister's handling of Cabinet and the changing role of the Cabinet Office are two highly contentious issues that will be examined from different perspectives in later chapters. We will begin our discussion by focusing on cabinet committees.

Cabinet committees

We have already given a brief overview of the history of cabinet committees in Chapter 1 so we will begin immediately to analyse them in more detail. Cabinet committees are the responsibility of the Prime Minister. It is the Prime Minister who will establish the committee, give it its terms of reference and appoint its chair and members.

Cabinet committees were introduced, and have developed alongside, the massive growth in the volume and complexity of modern government. Before the 1970s government regularly denied the existence of these committees. It was not until the publication of ministerial diaries in the 1970s that cabinet committees became common knowledge outside the confines of Whitehall and Parliament. Even then, an official announcement on the number and nature of these committees had to wait until 1992 when John Major finally went public and published details of the whole structure.

Why cabinet committees exist

Cabinet committees are at the very heart of the British executive. The use of the word 'heart' is a common metaphor when describing these particular elements of government, and we will soon get an impression of this 'heart' of government as a fairly crowded place. This realisation should strengthen the view we are developing here of a cabinet 'system' of government that embraces many more actors and institutions than would have been involved in 1916.

The majority of the decisions taken 'by the Cabinet' are, in effect, taken by cabinet committees. Cabinet committees provide a framework for collective consideration of, and decisions on, major policy issues and issues of significant public interest. They ensure that there is a proper discussion of issues that are of interest to more than one department and that all relevant ministers have their views considered. Committees will meet physically to resolve disputes and to make difficult decisions, yet may use correspondence to deal with less contentious issues.

The Cabinet Office website summarises the main business of cabinet committees in three broad spheres:

- The co-ordination of particularly complex government business such as the legislative programme, constitutional issues and public expenditure.
- Consideration of major issues of policy or issues likely to lead to significant public comment or criticism.
- Questions where there is an unresolved disagreement between departments.

Cabinet committees provide a useful overload facility for the full Cabinet by settling business and disputes in a smaller forum and at a lower level. They have an important link with collective responsibility in the way that they allow decisions to be considered fully by those ministers most closely concerned. It is this aspect of their function that ensures government as a whole can be expected to accept responsibility for the decisions that emerge.

If we turn to the role of cabinet committees in the decision-making process, then their importance becomes even clearer. Even in those instances where the committee has not taken a decision itself, it is highly likely that the crucial debates prior to a higher-level decision will already have taken place in the committee. Cabinet committees are shadowed by committees of civil servants and prepare papers for their discussion, and it is now largely accepted that decisions taken in cabinet committees have the same status as Cabinet decisions. This situation has been formalised by allowing all cabinet committees to act by a device known as '**implied devolution**'. This means they are given their authority and legitimacy by the full Cabinet and that their decisions have the same formal status as those taken by the full Cabinet. Only on those occasions when the committee has been unable to reach a decision will the issue find its way on to the higher Cabinet agenda. While committee chairs are allowed to take disputes to the full Cabinet (though they are discouraged from doing so), Treasury ministers defeated in committee over public spending have had, since 1975, automatic right of appeal to the Cabinet.

Structure of cabinet committees

When John Major finally threw back the veil from around the cabinet committee system, he did no more than reveal what political journalists and academics had been able to work out for themselves: a system of committees of various kinds, some with subcommittees that tend to focus on narrower issues than those dealt with by the full committee. We can now identify four types of cabinet committee:

- **Standing** – permanent for the duration of the Prime Minister's term in office.
- **Miscellaneous, or *ad hoc*** – set up to deal with particular issues.
- **Official committees** – consist only of civil servants.
- **Ministerial groups** – a new addition to the committee system in 1998. These tend to be less formal and have a wider membership that is not exclusive to cabinet members. Recent ministerial groups have chosen to focus on Food Safety and Rural Issues, Genetic Modification and Crime Reduction. These types of group were a response to the desire of 'new' Labour in the late 1990s to produce 'joined-up' and more co-ordinated government.

In May 2005, the Cabinet Office website was also referring to the existence of **consultative committees** where matters are discussed with others outside the British government. Examples provided by the Cabinet Office included the Joint Consultative Committee with the Liberal Democrats and the Joint Ministerial Committee with the devolved administrations. The relationship between these two committees and the rest of the cabinet committee structure is not clear. Neither of them appears on the Cabinet Office web-pages that list the committees of the cabinet. The main focus of the website is on the ministerial and the miscellaneous/*ad hoc* committees and provides links to their terms of reference. A full list of cabinet committees as they appeared in the summer of 2005 will be reproduced later in this chapter. You should also note the large number of subcommittees that the system has now produced.

The role of cabinet committees

In research published as part of the 'Whitehall Programme',[1] Brady and Catterall suggest that cabinet committees have two main purposes. The following table is a summary of their key arguments:

Brady and Caterall go on to point out that the familiar division of cabinet committees along the lines of those set out above do not correspond to the roles in Table 3.1. The difference between those

Table 3.1 The purpose of cabinet committees

Political purpose – to provide political support to the Cabinet, particularly on Sensitive on controversial issues	**Administrative purpose** – to co-ordinate policy and clear the ground for legislation. Committees have four main administrative roles
• Cabinet does not have to discuss everything. Not all issues are equally important. Committees can deal with these 'lesser' issues. • Controversy and confrontation may be 'side tracked' out of the Cabinet. • A newly set-up committee can achieve the twin tasks of doing the preparatory work for a new policy while satisfying the public demand that 'something should be done'.	• To advise Cabinet on scenarios, options and technical detail. • Policy formulation – preparing policy or legislation. • Executive decision making – this may not involve approval from the Cabinet. • Implementing policy and overseeing the introduction into departments.

committees considered to be 'standing' and those considered to be 'ad hoc' are usually decided by how long the committee will be required to sit and what breadth of reference it is given. As we shall see when we examine the cabinet committees under Blair, crises frequently generate *ad hoc* committees that may or may not evolve into the standing variety. This is a strength rather than a weakness of the system. The distinction between *ad hoc* and standing and between official and ministerial suggests a very flexible and responsive set-up that can adapt to a quickly changing political atmosphere. The fact that a special committee for consultation with the Liberal Party on Constitutional Reform was set up after 1997 illustrates the fluid and positive aspects of the cabinet committee system that is capable of 'accommodating so many different inputs'. Ian Budge refers to this joint cabinet committee as a 'harbinger of important change for all sorts of reasons'.[2] These changes associated with this unique experiment in British government included:

- Showing a break with the constitutional convention of majority party dominance and total confrontation with the opposition.
- Keeping constitutional reform firmly on the political agenda.
- Providing a political device for the Prime Minister to put pressure on traditionalists within the Cabinet who oppose change.

Cabinet committees and policy

Having established the fact that cabinet committees have become central to decision making in the years since 1945 and that much of what cabinet committees decide does not need formal Cabinet approval it is nevertheless important to consider their role in the policy-making process in more detail. As we have already seen, a cabinet committee is able to fulfil a number of tasks. Once these tasks are complete, and at the end of the process a decision emerges, it is the job of the Cabinet Office to distribute these decisions to the relevant departments in government. It is the departments that must then implement these decisions. The role that a cabinet committee takes in the policy-making process depends very much on the way that different prime ministers use the system yet also allows considerable flexibility to the ministers who chair these committees and those ministers who sit on more than one of them. According to Burch, decisions reached in cabinet committees may represent what he refers to as 'the points at which major policies are determined and decided'.[3] It is possible to draw attention to a number of policies which, although considered in committee, required a decision in full Cabinet. These include:

- Reform of the National Health Service (1988–9).
- The replacement of the local Poll Tax by the new Council Tax (1991).
- The incorporation of the European Convention on Human Rights into British law (1997 – although final implementation was later).
- The introduction and level of a national minimum wage (1998 – but again, implemented later).

Occasionally, Cabinet will ask committees to look again at the recommendations that they are making or may refer the issue further back down the policy-making line. We can highlight two examples to illustrate this point:

- The Freedom of Information Act (1998). Both Prime Minister and Home Secretary were unhappy with the recommendations from committee.
- Plans to privatise the Post Office (1993). Major and the majority of his Cabinet felt that Heseltine's proposals would not be approved by Parliament.

Cabinet committees under Thatcher and Major

Margaret Thatcher appears not to have favoured cabinet committees and, as a result, created relatively few of them. Compare Attlee's use of the committees with that of Thatcher:

- Attlee, 1945–51: 148 standing, 313 *ad hoc*.
- Thatcher, 1979–87: 35 standing, 120 *ad hoc*.

Full Cabinet fared little better under Thatcher to the extent that almost 50 per cent fewer cabinet meetings were being held in 1990 than in 1970. Rather than utilise the full cabinet system, Thatcher preferred instead to seek **'bilateral'** meetings with ministers and officials or would set up a 'working party' to tackle a particular problem.

Table 3.2 Ministerial (standing) committees of the Cabinet (May 2005)

Committee	Subcommittees
Antisocial Behaviour	
Asylum and Migration	
Civil Contingencies	
Constitutional Affairs	Electoral Policy
	Freedom of Information
	Parliamentary Modernisation
Intelligence Services	
Defence and Overseas Policy	International Terrorism
	Protective Security and Resilience
	Iraq
	Conflict Prevention / Reconstruction
Domestic Affairs	Ageing Policy
	Children's Policy
	Communities
	Legal Affairs
	Public Health
Economic Affairs	
Energy and the Environment	Sustainable Development
European Policy	
European Union Strategy	
Housing and Planning	
Legislative Programme	
Local and Regional Government	Local Government Strategy
NHS Reform	
Public Service and Expenditure	Electronic Service Delivery
Public Services Reform	
Regulation, Bureaucracy and Risk	Regulatory Accountability
	Inspection
Schools Policy	
Science	
Serious and Organised Crime and Drugs	
Welfare Reform	

Under Major, both the Cabinet and the cabinet committee system were restored to something resembling the 'normality' of the pre-Thatcher savaging even though the general trend away from the Cabinet continued. In an attempt not to repeat wholesale the mistakes of his predecessor, Major tried wherever he could to include as many ministers as possible in the relevant discussions and key decision-making moments. Major also tended to make better use of ministerial standing committees even if the *ad hoc* committees were used even less frequently than they had been under Thatcher. The consequence of this fall in the number of committees and the frequency of their meetings is not necessarily a negative development as it has led to a more streamlined and regularised cabinet committee system. The system has continued to exist and evolve under Tony Blair, to whom we may now turn.

Tony Blair and cabinet committees

As we are able to see from the following table, the number of cabinet committees under Blair has increased. In June 2005, the following ministerial cabinet committees could be viewed in detail on the appropriate government website.

Table 3.3 shows the *ad hoc* or miscellaneous committees.

It has been pointed out that, under Blair, though the number of committees has increased, the use of them has tended to be somewhat erratic. In the first Blair government, key cabinet committees met regularly to discuss policy themes central to the original 'New' Labour programme. These issues included devolution legislation, incorporation of the European Convention, freedom of information and House of Lords reform. They were also set up to deal with military issues in Afghanistan, Kosovo and Iraq. In his biography of Blair, Seldon attributes part of Blair's lack of enthusiasm for cabinet committees as an illustration of his general lack of trust in the Civil Service machine as a whole.[4] One senior adviser confided to Seldon that Blair had no time for cabinet committees because he felt 'they

Table 3.3 *Ad hoc*/miscellaneous committees (May 2005)

Restructuring of the European Space and Defence Industry
Animal Rights Activists
Universal Banking
Olympics
London
Efficiency and Relocation

just went round and round in circles and did nothing'. Other members of the government made more use of them, especially Brown and Prescott. According to James Naughtie, however, Brown ultimately had less time for the committee system than Blair, even though the Prime Minister had given his Chancellor the chair of the 'prize' Committee on Economic Affairs. This large committee, which includes all the ministers with the big Whitehall budgets, is one of the two most important sub-Cabinet groups, alongside the Defence and Overseas Policy Committee. The significance of Brown being given the chair of this committee is important only in the recognition that no Chancellor had been allowed to do so since Wilson took control of it for himself in 1966. Although this arrangement appears to have been part of the infamous 'deal' struck between Blair and Brown in opposition, the Chancellor has never developed or strengthened the committee. Like Blair, Brown appears to prefer to do his business elsewhere: 'Gordon at his grumpiest' is how a member of the committee described the Chancellor to Naughtie, 'He can't wait to get it over. Maybe that's why he's so rude to us.' A picture thus emerges of a man who would really rather be somewhere else, who prefers to listen to advisers rather than committee members and who spends most of his time in the meetings 'scribbling on piles of papers'.[5]

For Seldon, this attitude at the very top of the government towards cabinet committees is something of an irony. For an administration that has attempted to make a virtue of its intention to have 'joined-up' government, it has actually shunned some of the very mechanisms that have been 'ensuring joined-up government for a hunded years'. From within the Blair court itself, the view of cabinet committees has been slightly less critical. While acknowledging that bilateral and *ad hoc* meetings serviced by Number 10 staff are a 'good idea because they are small and manageable and bring together those with real interest and weight, who can reach decisions more rapidly', Peter Mandelson has argued that this style of government 'can happily coexist with the more formal cabinet committees'.[6]

How effective are cabinet committees?
When discussing the effectiveness of cabinet committees, we are drawn back to a consideration of the leadership style, approach and attitude of the Prime Minister. If a prime minister wishes to develop

a strong and well-resourced structure of cabinet committees that then beats away at the crucial heart of the government machine, then there is really nothing to stop him or her doing so; this was certainly the intention of David Lloyd George when he introduced them in 1916. As we have seen, attitudes towards the committee system differ from prime minister to prime minister. In recent years, the appointment of cabinet 'enforcers', who have generally tended to sit on the major committees, is another indicator of their general importance in the wider system of government. According to Brady and Catterall, the effectiveness of cabinet committees rests upon two requirements:

- The more effective committees display a clear relationship between the committee and the departments which actually implement policy.
- Secondly, effective committees will have a clear sense of political direction concerning the policy goals towards which the committee is working.

If these conditions are missing, then there is a real possibility that the committee, however important it might be, will either 'operate in a vacuum or degenerate into a talking shop'.[7] The description of Brown's chairing of the Economic Affairs Committee may well illustrate this particular point.

Other criticisms of the cabinet committee system include:

- Most major committees, both standing and *ad hoc*, are chaired by the Prime Minister. This simply adds fuel to the arguments that Blair can use committees as an extra means of political patronage and as yet another device with which to dominate Cabinet.
- The large number of committees makes it increasingly difficult for ministers to check effectively everything that is being decided prior to the decisions being ratified by Cabinet.
- A badly organised system of cabinet committees can lead to overlap and duplication of effort. This can lead to 'policy fragmentation'.
- Committees can become the venue for 'turf wars' between competing departments.
- It is not always the case that those people charged with the management and direction of the committee are always in charge. Brady and Catterall write of ministers who are not formal members

of a committee turning up more regularly, and making more of a contribution, than those who are supposed to be there.

• The Prime Minister is not always able to supply sufficiently clear political direction to committees. Without this, they are likely to be less successful.

• Regular restructuring of government departments and central government mechanisms frequently leave cabinet committees confused and adrift in a system that changes rapidly around them.

Irrespective of the above criticisms and shortcomings of cabinet committees, they remain an integral part of the government machinery. There are several key points to make in their favour by way of concluding this section:

• They allow small groups of ministers to focus on very specific and specialised decision making.

• They provide the opportunity to invite outsiders with specific knowledge or critical opinions into the decision-making process.

• They provide a fail-safe mechanism for policy/decision making in the event of the Prime Minister not being up to the job.

It might be useful at this point to review your notes on cabinet committees or attempt some of the questions at the end of this chapter that will test your understanding and knowledge of this key element of cabinet government. We can now move on and look in more detail at the real bureaucracy that underpins the functioning of cabinet government as a whole by assessing the origins and functions of the Cabinet Office.

The Cabinet Office

If the Cabinet and its various committees are at the heart of the government machine then the Cabinet Office represents the valves and chambers of the heart in the way that it directs crucial information and paperwork throughout the arteries of central government. The modern Cabinet Office has three key functions:

• To prepare the agenda of the Cabinet.
• To record Cabinet decisions and proceedings.
• To check and monitor appropriate actions.

Evolution of the Cabinet Office

The Cabinet Office was established by Lloyd George in 1916. Prior to this, Cabinet would meet and take decisions yet have no record of what it had discussed or decided nor did it have any real idea as to how and when the decisions would be acted upon. From the outset, a major part of the Cabinet Office has been the Cabinet Secretariat which is headed by the Cabinet Secretary and has a staff of around 2,000.

Structure of the modern Cabinet Office

The Cabinet Office is headed by the Cabinet Secretary and is situated at 10 Downing Street. It is appropriate to think of the Cabinet Office as being organised and structured on two levels – the administrative and the political. This is an important distinction and we will return to it shortly.

Modern government requires a huge administrative backup. We have already discussed the size of the Cabinet and the number of cabinet committees and subcommittees, and it should be clear that this system generates large numbers of meetings which, in turn, require agendas, papers for discussion, minutes of meetings, and must then process the decisions that are made. The whole system will also require huge numbers of memorandums and other forms of communication to keep all key ministers, committees and groups informed of the formulation, general direction, and implementation of government policy. We have also noted in the section earlier in this chapter how every cabinet committee is shadowed by an official committee of civil servants who do much of the preparatory work on which ministers will rely to make their final decisions. These official committees have specialist knowledge of complex policy areas (especially those relating to Europe) and are also organised by the Cabinet Office. Most of this administrative work is done by assistant secretaries. An assistant secretary is a fairly senior official who will be temporarily seconded to the Cabinet Office from other departments. They normally stay at Number 10 for approximately two to three years. These administrative and secretarial posts are also referred to as the **Cabinet Secretariat**, and form a major part of the Cabinet Office. According to the Cabinet Office website:

The Cabinet Secretariat is non-departmental in function and purpose. It services the Cabinet itself together with its Cabinet Committees and subcommittees. The Secretariat aims to ensure that the business of government is conducted in a timely and efficient way and that proper consideration takes place when it is needed before policy decisions are taken.

The role of the Cabinet Secretariat is crucial to the general organisation of the government. It is not the case, however, that the work of the Secretariat can always be considered politically neutral. Agendas drawn up by the Secretariat can be written and organised in such a way that can influence the length and nature of the discussions that will take place. This type of influence could also be extended to the preparation of minutes that may be written in such a way as to prefer one line of discussion to another. This may be an attempt to influence the final decision towards a particular policy when discussed at a higher level. The minutes of cabinet meetings themselves are a particularly good example of this as they are written by the Cabinet Secretary in consultation with the Prime Minister and form the official policy decisions of the government.

We have already mentioned that the Cabinet Secretary is the head of the Civil Service, and it is worth taking some time now to consider this point in more detail. As head of the Civil Service, the Cabinet Secretary is in charge of the conduct and conditions of service for Whitehall as a whole. This aspect of the post means that he or she will be the person to preside over all reforms to the Civil Service. Although we shall soon concentrate on reforms under Tony Blair, it is worth mentioning that the Civil Service was also subjected to considerable reforms in the 1980s. Some of these reforms were unpopular and controversial; many of those instigated by Thatcher, for instance, fundamentally changed the structure and working practices of Whitehall. The high-profile nature of such reforms has frequently thrust the Cabinet Secretary into a degree of public exposure that holders of the post have not always found comfortable.

It is not just internal reforms, however, that have raised the profile of the Cabinet Secretary. Sir Robert Armstrong, for instance, was forced into the open during the 1980s to deal with an attempt by the government to ban the publication of *Spycatcher*, a book written by an ex-MI5 agent, and Armstrong was also drawn into the Westland Helicopters dispute that we have explained in some detail elsewhere.

It was suggested in the introduction to this section that the Cabinet Office and Secretariat are best viewed as being organised and structured on two levels – the administrative and the political. We have already given examples of how the workings of the Cabinet Office could be interpreted in a covertly political manner but we should now move on to discuss the more overt political role of both Office and Secretariat.

One of the key arguments that is being developed through this book is that the organisation and functions of the central executive are determined to a large extent by the style and direction of the Prime Minister. The extent to which the Cabinet Office, the Cabinet Secretary and the Secretariat act in a political way will vary from government to government. It is important to remember, of course, that none of the individuals or groups under discussion should have any political role at all. The Civil Service, you will recall, is expected, constitutionally to be politically neutral. The reality, as we shall see, is somewhat different.

While a minister such as Richard Crossman in the 1960s felt that Harold Wilson and his Cabinet Secretary, Sir Burke Trend, spent far too long 'massaging' the minutes of cabinet meetings, it was the period of government under Margaret Thatcher when concerns began to be raised on a regular basis over her use of the Office to help her control both the Civil Service and the Cabinet. Speculation about the political role of the Cabinet Office and Secretariat has increased substantially in the Blair administrations. The nature of the Cabinet Office under Blair will be considered in the following section. To summarise the key arguments and criticisms, however, we could say that Blair has used the Cabinet Office as follows:

- It has become his direct instrument of control over government.
- He has used it to modernise the government machine.
- He has placed it at the centre of a new machinery of committees, commissions and working groups which are developing policy on current issues that are not the individual responsibility of departments. You can check this by looking again at the list of 'ministerial' cabinet committees in the table earlier in this chapter.

- It has become an extension of the Prime Minister's Office, especially where it is concerned with policy presentation.

In essence, the Cabinet Office undertakes a huge and complicated role of co-ordination. In recent years, the nature of the Cabinet Office has come under much scrutiny, and claims have been made that it has now become a 'Prime Minister's Department' in all but name.

Blair and the Cabinet Office

Following the election of the Labour government in 1997, the Cabinet Office was divided into four smaller secretariats:

- Economic and Domestic Affairs
- Defence and Overseas
- European (European Union)
- Constitution

These four secretariats were accountable to the Prime Minister through the Cabinet Secretary and to ministers who chaired committees. The Economic and Domestic Secretariat dealt with legislative and parliamentary matters. The Constitution Secretariat co-ordinated work on constitutional reform including devolution to Scotland, Wales and the English regions and the incorporation into British law of the European Convention on Human Rights.

When Sir Richard Wilson was appointed as Cabinet Secretary in January 1998, Blair asked him to draw up plans to strengthen the Cabinet Office. His report was completed by Easter 1998 and then delayed to coincide with Blair's first cabinet reshuffle. When the reshuffle was finally announced in July 1998 Blair took the opportunity to announce his changes to the Cabinet Office. The changes took place in seven key areas:

- The Cabinet Office was placed under the control of a cabinet minister – Jack Cunningham – who was given the 'strategic' responsibility to drive Blair's agenda in Whitehall. The press immediately used the term 'Cabinet Enforcer' to describe this new post.
- A **Performance and Innovation Unit** was set up inside the Cabinet Office – this was a particularly powerful innovation.

- The head of Government Information and Communications Service and the government's Chief Scientific Adviser were to be based inside the Cabinet Office.
- The Women's Unit was to be relocated and based inside the Cabinet Office.
- A **Centre for Management and Policy Studies** was to be set up to ensure that officials were trained in the latest management techniques.
- Staff from the seventeen existing Cabinet Office buildings were to be moved to the Cabinet Office in Downing Street.
- The Office of Public Service was to be merged with the rest of the Cabinet Office.

Two of these reforms are worth looking at in more detail. The **'Cabinet Enforcer'**, placed in charge of the Cabinet Office, reflected some of Blair's frustration experienced during his first year in office – 'one of the most frustrating things about coming into government is the time it takes to get stuff moving through the system'.[8] Cunningham went to some length to send a clear message to the Civil Service that it was the intention that he would work with Sir Richard Wilson as a 'joint partner'. According to Cunningham, the Cabinet Office had to adapt to being more than just the 'powerful engine of government'. In future, thought Cunningham, the Cabinet Office would be involved in 'key policy initiatives . . . if problems are looming, it's my responsibility to make Blair aware of them'.

The **Performance and Innovation Unit** was staffed by civil servants and experts recruited for short stints to review specific policies. The first priorities handed down from Blair included the development of policies on older people, cities and the regions. Some observers have interpreted the setting up of this unit as one of the first signs of tension between Tony Blair and Gordon Brown. The Treasury already monitored departmental programmes and provided an overview of government policy. John Rentoul, one of Blair's early biographers, interpreted this as an 'unacknowledged tussle . . . Brown as the Chief Executive under 'chairman' Blair'.[9]

After the 2001 general election the Cabinet Office was placed under the control of the Deputy Prime Minister, and a number of new special offices and units was brought within it. These included:

- The **Office of Public Service Reform** was set up to oversee the implementation of the government's reform programme.
- The **Delivery Unit** was set up to monitor and improve policy delivery. This was to be regarded by most observers as the most successful of the post-2001 election reforms.
- The **Forward Strategy Unit** was designed to give a clear focus on working up policy from first principles ('blue sky thinking') and was largely the brainchild of John Birt who had stressed to Blair the importance of strategic thinking.

To a large extent, the 2001 reforms mark Blair's 'last chance' (Seldon) to 'get things right'. In the context of that particular ambition, the Delivery Unit would prove to be Blair's main control mechanism to ensure that improvements happened as promised in the second term. Taken as a package, the reforms constituted nothing less than a revolution in the workings of Number 10 and in the relationship between Number 10 and the Cabinet Office.

Following the appointment of Sir Andrew Turnbull as the new Cabinet Secretary in 2002, a further reorganisation brought together these reform and delivery units that started in the Cabinet Office into a single integrated structure. The reorganised Cabinet Office was to focus its work on four key objectives:

- To support the Prime Minister in leading the government.
- To support the Cabinet in transacting its business.
- To lead and support the reform and delivery programme.
- To co-ordinate security and intelligence.

We shall look at the significance of these reforms more closely in Chapter 6 when we consider in detail the significance of the structural changes to the Cabinet Office made since 1997. To give some indication of the direction of our discussion on this particular issue, it is worth noting that Peter Hennessey has argued that, under Blair, there has been a fusion of the Prime Minister's Office and the Cabinet Office as resources for the Prime Minister, and that this has rendered obsolete the debate over a Prime Minister's Department.[10] We will also mention elsewhere the continued reorganisation of the Cabinet Office after the 2002 reshuffle caused by the resignation of Stephen Byers, the Transport Secretary. The Deputy Prime Minister was moved from the Cabinet Office into a separate and expanded Deputy Prime Minister's Department. The Cabinet Office, under Lord Macdonald, reported directly to Tony Blair, thus providing extra evidence to support the views of observers like Hennessey who argue that the Cabinet Office is now a resource for the Prime Minister rather than for the Cabinet as a whole.

....

✔ What you should have learnt from reading this chapter

The bureaucracy and support mechanisms of the modern Cabinet are complex and subject to a gradual process of reform and change. Some of these reforms have raised concerns about the nature of the support systems now available and in particular the possible politicisation of the offices involved. A number of the themes and issues that have been raised here will be revisited when we consider the powers and role of the Prime Minister in more detail.

🔎 Glossary of key terms

Bilateral meetings A device favoured by Margaret Thatcher and Tony Blair that involves one-to-one meetings on specific issues with relevant ministers as opposed to discussing the issue in full Cabinet.
Cabinet committees Appointed by the Prime Minister to deal with items of government business. Discussions in committee are supposed to inform decisions in full Cabinet. In June, 2005, including subcommittees, there were around forty-two cabinet committees.
Cabinet enforcer The term first used to describe the Labour MP Jack Cunningham who was given control of the Cabinet Office in an attempt to streamline the delivery of policy.
Cabinet Office Prepares the agendas and minutes of the Cabinet. Plays an important role in co-ordinating the work of government.
Cabinet Secretariat The administrative and secretarial posts that form a major part of the Cabinet Office.

❓ Likely examination questions

Short questions

Describe the origins and functions of cabinet committees.

Identify and describe four types of cabinet committee.

Explain the role of the Cabinet Office.

Describe the key functions of the Cabinet Secretariat.

Briefly describe the reforms to the Cabinet Office introduced by Tony Blair.

Essay questions

To what extent would you agree with the suggestion that cabinet committees have replaced collective cabinet government?

'Cabinet committees are an effective means of organising modern government.' How far do you agree with this suggestion?

To what extent and in what ways has Tony Blair changed the role and structure of the Cabinet Office?

'The Cabinet Office is now the Prime Minister's Department.' Discuss.

Revision task

Use an A3 sheet of paper to draw a diagram that shows the following:

• The current structure of Cabinet Committees.

• The current structure of the Cabinet Office.

• You could also attempt to show the links between the two.

 ## Helpful websites

www.number10.gov.uk/

www.direct.gov.uk/

www.cabinetoffice.gov.uk/

Make good use of this in the revision task.

www.civilservice.gov.uk

 ## Suggestions for further reading

Brady, C. and Catterall, P. (2000) 'Inside the Engine Room: Assessing Cabinet Committees', *Talking Politics*, vol. 12.3, spring 2000.

Budge, I. (ed.) (2000) *New British Politics* (Longman).

Burch, M. and Halliday, I. (1996) *The British Cabinet System* (Prentice Hall).

Hennessy, P. (1998) 'The Blair Style of Government', *Government and Opposition*, winter 1997–8.

Jones, B (ed.) (2004) *Politics UK*, 5th edn (Longman Pearson), chapter 19.

McNaughton, N. (1999) *The Prime Minister and Cabinet Government* (Hodder), chapters 2 and 3.

McNaughton, N. (2001) *Success in Politics*, 2nd edn (Murray), Unit 8.

Mandelson, P. (2002) *The Blair Revolution Revisited* (Politico's).

Naughtie, J. (2002) *The Rivals* (Fourth Estate).

Rathbone, M. (2003) 'The British Cabinet Today', *Talking Politics*, vol. 16.1, September 2003.

Rentoul, J. (2001) *Tony Blair: Prime Minister* (Time Warner).

Seldon, A. (2004) *Blair* (Free Press).

Thomas, G. (1998) *Prime Minister and Cabinet Today* (Manchester University Press).

Thomas, G. (2002) 'The Prime Minister and Cabinet', *Politics Review,* vol. 11.4, 2002.

CHAPTER 4

The Cabinet: Collectively Dead?

Contents

Overview

In this chapter, we move on to examine the current state of the Cabinet. In recent years the doctrine of collective cabinet responsibility has received substantial scrutiny from politicians, political commentators and academics alike. Under the leadership of Tony Blair, the British cabinet system has been subjected to some particularly close criticisms that have been illuminated by the spotlights offered by the Iraq war in general and the related issue of the Hutton Inquiry in particular.

Key issues to be covered in this chapter

- Definitions and traditional views of how the doctrine of collective responsibility came into being and is supposed to work
- The impact of recent events, especially those surrounding the war in Iraq, on the condition of cabinet government
- The debate surrounding the 'decline' of cabinet government

Introduction

Collective cabinet responsibility refers to the accepted conduct of government ministers as part of the Cabinet. Under this doctrine, ministers are bound to support publicly the decisions made by Cabinet as a whole and will show no disagreement with these decisions outside of the cabinet room. The doctrine has evolved as a means of maintaining the appearance of Cabinet unity and party discipline and showing that the government is firmly behind the policies it promotes and seeks to pass through Parliament.

A more critical definition of the doctrine may be offered, however. The doctrine of collective cabinet responsibility evolved as a means of giving a public appearance of Cabinet unity and genuine collective decision making. The notion that ministers all accept the constraints of this doctrine, and are therefore bound by it, is increasingly difficult to accept. There are, in recent years, examples of cabinet ministers willing to break free from the constraints of a doctrine that binds them to decisions they do not agree with. The doctrine also requires review given the ongoing debates surrounding the nature of prime ministerial government and the relationship between the first minister and those appointed to ministerial positions.

In a recent (November 2004) House of Commons research paper on the collective responsibility of ministers, Gay and Powell began their analysis by stating that the convention of collective Cabinet, or ministerial, responsibility is at the heart of the British system of parliamentary government yet, like individual responsibility, it is a concept that is not regulated by statute, although some guidance has been formalised in the Ministerial Code. They went on to say that: 'Collective responsibility serves to bind the government together so that it faces the monarch, Parliament and the public united. Yet, as with individual responsibility, the operation of this concept must depend as much, if not more, on political reality as on constitutional convention.'[1] The notion of collective cabinet responsibility is clearly a debatable issue in British politics and one that this chapter will seek to investigate in detail.

Collective cabinet responsibility

The doctrine of collective cabinet responsibility is not unique to politics. Most people who join together in pursuit of some shared goal or aim – sports clubs, for example – have to be prepared to accept the rules and regulations of the groups, especially if they serve on the organising committees. When promoted to the Cabinet, ministers are given a document, *Questions for the Procedures of Ministers*, which, among other things, sets out the rules for the workings of collective responsibility. All prime ministers produce a version of this document which will cover all aspects of ministerial procedures, including everything from collective responsibility to the publication of *memoirs*. The original version, first drawn up by Attlee in 1945, consisted of four pages and twenty-three paragraphs. In his book *Arguments for Democracy* the ex-Labour minister, Tony Benn, referred to the 1976 version of the document recently released under the thirty-year rule that had grown to twenty-seven pages and included a separate minute relating to travel. These documents are not submitted to the Cabinet for approval and the Prime Minister is able to prevent any discussion of their contents.[2] For critics such as Benn the rules regarding the application, or non-application, of collective responsibility are entirely within the personal discretion of the Prime Minister, as some of the examples we shall use here will show.

While the debate over collective cabinet responsibility is not particularly new, the concept itself has a much longer history. Collective responsibility was developed among groups of Ministers in the eighteenth and nineteenth centuries as a way of seizing political control from the monarch. Once again, Walpole provides us with our starting point. Having established the principal of cabinet government, the first prime minister recognised that, for the system to work effectively, there had to be the acceptance of group discipline among the group of ministers chosen collectively to run the country. Collective cabinet responsibility may therefore be traced back to the early eighteenth century and has been a key part of the British Constitution ever since.

The three strands of the convention
Geoffrey Marshall has highlighted three individual strands within the convention of collective responsibility.[3] The table below summarises these three strands:

Gay and Powell use these broad principles to suggest four key ways in which the three strands may be applied in practical circumstances, albeit with varying degrees of constitutional certainty:

Table 4.1 Three strands of collective responsibility

Confidence	Unanimity	Confidentiality
• Government will only remain in power for as long as it retains the confidence of the House of Commons.	• All members of the government speak and vote together in Parliament – unless where an exception is made.	• Discussion in Cabinet must be confidential if open and frank exchanges of views are to take place.
• Confidence is always assumed unless a confidence vote is lost by the government.	• The universal application of unanimity may well be a 'constitutional fiction'.	• Unanimity may be a 'fiction', but confidentiality must be maintained.

- **Ministers must not vote against government policy** – without this, it could be argued that a government has lost the right to exist, and is therefore the most fundamental part of the whole doctrine of collective cabinet responsibility. When a minister votes for his or her government, he/she is giving a public expression of support even though, in private, he or she may be less enthusiastic for the measure. Even an abstention would be seen as breaking the convention – it is not enough simply not to vote against, but a positive display of support is required.
- **Ministers must not speak against government policy** – voting against or abstaining are fairly clear breaches of the convention, yet speaking against the government is less clear-cut. In the age of spin, press briefings and leaks, a minister may always find a way to communicate his or her dissatisfaction with a particular government position. Given what we shall shortly discuss when we consider the case of Clare Short, it is fair to say that the situation has changed considerably from the days when it was safe to assert that ministers who were not prepared to defend a cabinet position had no alternative but to resign.
- **All decisions are decisions of the whole government** – and a minister should not brief or leak against a cabinet colleague

in order to attack the position of an individual or group within Cabinet or to place distance between themselves and the policy. One of the more obvious examples of this particular flaw in the convention may be observed by a closer examination of the Westland Helicopters affair of 1986.

- **A former minister must not reveal cabinet secrets** – although there are certainly ways of working around this. It has become the tradition in recent years that ministers who resign make resignation speeches in the Commons. These can have an impact of varying degrees. Sir Geoffrey Howe, for instance, was able to deliver a devastating resignation speech with significant implications for Margaret Thatcher in 1990. Robin Cook was able to deliver a similarly devastating resignation speech in 2003. The reasons for resignation that are set out in these speeches often come close to revealing cabinet secrets and have serious consequences for the Prime Minister and government as outlined in the two examples here. The formal exchange of resignation letters can be similarly revealing. The other issue relating to this fourth application includes ministerial memoirs and autobiographies. The majority of senior politicians can now expect to be tempted with generous publishing deals soon after their departure from office. The nature of the Crossman diaries in the 1970s provided one of the first tests of this application, and the published diaries, memoirs and autobiographies of former ministers continue to do so.

Challenges and breaches

Having established some clear definitions of the doctrine of collective cabinet responsibility, it should be apparent that it is not the case that the principle has never been challenged or that exemptions have never been allowed. This section offers a brief summary of those occasions when the doctrine has been the subject of both. Challenges and breaches may be summarised under five key subheadings:

- Agreements to differ
- Free votes
- Splits and resignations
- Leaks
- Memoirs

We shall begin by providing examples of 'agreements to differ'. These, along with 'free votes', represent the formal mechanism of suspending collective cabinet responsibility:

The national government and tariff policy – 1932
This particular example illustrates what we may refer to as an **'agreement to differ'**. In 1932, during a period of coalition 'national' government between the Conservative Party and its partners, a major disagreement arose around the issue of tariff reform. During the 1931 general election campaign, coalition candidates made an agreement not to stand in opposition to each other even though there were clear splits over tariffs. After the election, four members of the Cabinet refused to accept the decision to impose a general tariff, and made it known that they would resign. The Labour leader and Prime Minister, Ramsay MacDonald, made the four members an offer that they would be allowed to disagree with the tariff reform in public if they would stay in the Cabinet. The four rebels went one step further and demanded they be given the freedom to speak against and vote against any tariff proposals and that MPs be given the same freedom. They also demanded that government whips be warned off applying any pressure to ministers to get them to support the government line. MacDonald agreed to this and the Cabinet was therefore freed from usual practice. This 'modification of usual ministerial practice' allowed those members of the Cabinet who could not support the 'conclusions of the majority' to express their views by speech and vote. The whole 'agreement to differ' was justified on the grounds that, in difficult times (it was the height of the Depression), such a departure from the norm allowed for the best means of 'interpreting the will of the nation and the needs of the time'.

Views on the 'agreement' were mixed. Those opposing it pointed out that there could be no such thing as a 'collective conscience' while others took the view that the British Constitution was a 'living organism' capable of change and flexibility. Stanley Baldwin came to the rather neat conclusion that 'we have collective responsibility for the departure from collective action'. It should be noted here that, under a national government, the accepted constitutional conventions were sometimes difficult to apply. The national government was not 'party' government in the way we understand the term in 'normal' circumstances, and therefore contemporary commentators recognised what was happening in 1932 was very much a product of, if not unique to, the certainly unusual political circumstances.

Labour and the EEC referendum – 1975

Wilson's Cabinet was removed from the constraints of collective responsibility during the 1975 referendum on continued British membership of the European Economic Community. Labour came to power in 1974 with a pledge to renegotiate the terms of the United Kingdom treaty and to allow the outcome to be voted on by the people, either in a general election or a referendum. The need for an 'agreement to differ' was raised by three senior members of the Cabinet – Peter Shore, Michael Foot and Tony Benn – who pointed out to Harold Wilson that the strength of views in the Cabinet was such that the these 'deep convictions cannot be shelved or set aside by the normal process of Cabinet decision-making'. Wilson announced on 23 January 1975 that a referendum would be held before the end of June that year; his statement to the Commons explained how the government would make its position on continued membership known when the outcome of the renegotiations was clear. The statement went on to say, however, that:

> The circumstances of the referendum are unique, and the issue to be decided is one on which strong views have long been held which cross party lines. The Cabinet has, therefore, decided that, if when the time comes there are members of the government, including members of the Cabinet, who do not feel able to accept and support the Government's recommendation; whatever it may be, they will, once the recommendation has been announced, be free to support and speak in favour of a different conclusion in the referendum campaign.

At this point, the uproar in the House is reported in Hansard by a simple 'Oh!'

Labour and the European Assembly direct elections – 1977

Wilson's policy in 1974 was repeated by his successor, James Callaghan, in 1977. Once again, Europe was the issue. The events of 1977 would prove to be much more complex than either 1932 or 1975, mainly because two issues were at stake: first, the principle of direct elections and, second, the voting method to be used. The situation was also confused because of the drawn-out nature of events that covered two parliamentary sessions and two bills.

In 1976, the United Kingdom had promised its 'best endeavours' to comply with an act of the Council of Foreign Ministers stating that member states should agree to try to implement legislation for direct elections to the European Assembly in spring 1978. The government did little to keep its promise and it was not until the events of March 1977, when Callaghan was forced into the 'Lib–Lab Pact' with the Liberals in order to preserve the Labour Party in office, that the issue resurfaced. As part of the deal with the Liberals the government restated its promise to legislate on direct elections and later promised that the issue would be the subject of a free vote in both houses of Parliament. Callaghan then announced to the Cabinet that there would also be a free vote for cabinet ministers on the issue. Callaghan will not be remembered as one of the most quotable of prime ministers, yet his response to Margaret Thatcher's questioning in the Commons about the suspension of collective cabinet responsibility is certainly worth repeating: 'Collective cabinet responsibility . . . I certainly think that the doctrine should apply, except in cases where I announce that it does not.'

Six cabinet ministers, along with twenty-five other members of the government, voted at the second reading against the bill to introduce a regional list system of voting. When a similar bill was introduced in the next session, the same six cabinet ministers now abstained from the vote, as did twenty other members of the government. The bill was finally passed as a guillotine motion even though four cabinet ministers defied a two-line whip.

The two examples cited in 1977, along with the 'agreement to differ' over tariffs in the 1932 national government represent the only occasions when the principle has been formally suspended. It is also worth mentioning **free votes** at this point. 'Free votes' are those occasions when there is no clear or stated government policy on the issue and, as a consequence, ministers cannot really be seen to dissent from any adopted policy. The most common use of free votes tends to be on questions with strong religious, social or moral connections. These kinds of issues have included abortion, capital punishment and gay rights. Free votes can often be much more than simply a device to give ministers the freedom not to compromise their consciences. They may be used when the party is split over an issue or wishes not to have to put forward a government line. The lack of government policy is the main distinction therefore between 'agreements to differ' and 'free votes'. We may turn now to those examples of the more unauthorised 'breaches' of collective responsibility. First, splits and resignations:

The Westland affair – 1986

This particular example could also be discussed in relation to cabinet 'leaks' (see below). In 1986 the then Conservative Defence Minister, Michael Heseltine, resigned from government over the issue of the purchase of helicopters. The British-owned Westland helicopter company was in severe financial difficulties and looked to be on the point of collapse. In the spirit of the time, this would normally have been seen as yet another company unable to manage itself effectively. Westland, however, was the main supplier of helicopters to the British armed forces and therefore its difficulties constituted a major crisis.

Heseltine argued strongly that Westland could be saved if it amalgamated with a European company. His cabinet colleague, Leon Brittan, the Secretary for Trade and Industry, however, argued instead that Westland should join with Sikorsky, an American company. At stake were a large number of British jobs and the principle of whether Britain should have closer defence links with America or with Europe. It also became clear to Heseltine that the Prime Minister, Margaret Thatcher, supported Leon Brittan and the American option. Unable to accept responsibility for a decision he did not feel had been properly discussed in Cabinet, Heseltine left the cabinet meeting to announce to the waiting press exactly what he had done. It was certainly one of the more theatrical illustrations of collective responsibility. At the same time, the Department of Trade leaked a letter from the Solicitor General that was very critical of the position taken by Michael Heseltine on the issue of how best to save the ailing helicopter company. This was a clear breach of ministerial confidentiality and one for which Brittan was eventually forced to resign.

Peter Dorey suggests that Heseltine's resignation is a prime example of the 'weakening' of collective responsibility through a much less stringent application of the doctrine.[4] Dorey goes on to suggest that Helseltine's claim that he was forced to resign was essentially a pretext to remove himself from government in order to make his bid for the leadership of the Conservative Party, not something he would have been able to do from within the Cabinet.

Geoffrey Howe and Europe – 1990

In a 1989 cabinet reshuffle, Geoffrey Howe had been demoted from the post of Foreign Secretary to Deputy Prime Minister. Rather than accept the demotion, Howe resigned and used his resignation speech, now free from the constraints of collective responsibility, to criticise the lack of genuine debate in Cabinet on Europe. The timing may also have been a pretext to force the Conservative Party into a serious leadership contest later that year.

The 'bastard' years – 1992–7

John Major headed a government that was in the process of tearing itself apart over the issue of Europe. The eurosceptics in the Cabinet, John Redwood, Peter Lilley, and Michael Portillo, all briefed against Major on European issues. When asked why he didn't simply sack them (they were clearly in breach of the doctrine of collective responsibility) Major made his famous reference to the problems caused by ex-ministers and did anyone really think he wanted 'three more of the bastards out there?'

Malcolm Chisholm – 1997

Chisholm resigned his position as a Scottish Office minister over the proposals by the Labour government to cut the lone-parent supplement to child benefit. This was unusual. A minister rarely finds it difficult to accept the first decision they do not agree with, certainly not to the point where they feel the need to free themselves from the collective responsibility and speak publicly. On this occasion, Chisholm was certainly reflecting the disquiet of many backbenchers in the Labour Party.

War in Iraq – 2003

British involvement in the war to topple the regime of Saddam Hussein in Iraq provides us with the most recent examples of questions surrounding the health of collective cabinet responsibility.

At the time of writing, the issue appears to have been responsible for several resignations, including two senior cabinet ministers – Robin Cook and Clare Short – and the criticism of an ex-minister on the back-benches, Mo Mowlam. These resignations will be the focus of a case study later in this chapter. Leaks and ministerial memoirs are the last two aspects of breaches of collective cabinet responsibility that we need to consider:

Leaks

To 'leak' information from the Cabinet is to pass unauthorised information to someone outside the Cabinet; more often than not, this person will be a journalist. Cabinet leaks break the convention of confidentiality that we outlined above. Leaks can often destroy the appearance of ministerial unanimity and can also compromise the secrecy of government. The 'unattributable leak', however, has now become established as a 'complement to the rigid precepts of collective responsibility', and leaks are the 'inevitable concomitant of collective responsibility'.[5] In other words, they are bound to happen and, even when they do (apart from two examples of budget leaks in 1936 and 1947), they rarely give away 'true' state secrets involving security, defence, devaluation or other budgetary matters. The Westland affair illustrates how ministers can avoid the rules of collective responsibility by leaking their views to the press and then denying any knowledge of the leak.

Memoirs and diaries

Should the restrictions of collective cabinet responsibility extend beyond the time served as a cabinet member? It is generally thought to be the case that the confidentiality of the Cabinet is a convention that does indeed extend into retirement. So, where does this leave the publication of ministerial memoirs?

Richard Crossman had been a member of Wilson's Cabinet in the 1960s and had kept a very detailed diary of his experiences. When extracts were published posthumously in the *Sunday Times* the Attorney-General sought injunctions against the newspaper to stop any further publications, even though the Cabinet Secretary had seen the extracts and made various deletions beforehand. After much legal wrangling, the case accepted the principle of a legal obligation of cabinet secrecy but that the application would depend on the time period involved between the cabinet meeting or decision and its eventual disclosure. Three rules eventually emerged from the 1976 Committee of Privy Councillors ('Radcliffe Report', 1976) which was established to consider the issue of ministerial memoirs:

- Ministers can describe and account for their opinions and actions but not those of others.
- Advice given by fellow cabinet ministers on civil servants should not be revealed.
- Judgements (favourable or otherwise) should not be made on those who served under the minister.

All former cabinet ministers who now wish to publish diaries or autobiographies are required to submit a typescript to the Cabinet Secretary first and to make sure that they stick to the three principles established by the 'Radcliffe Report'. For some observers, the growing number of ministerial diaries and memoirs is yet further evidence that cabinet confidentiality is no longer as secure as it once was.

The Case of Robin Cook and Clare Short

Robin Cook had been Foreign Secretary in the Labour government between 1997 and 2001. As Shadow Foreign Secretary he had promised that a Labour government would add an 'ethical dimension' to the conduct of foreign policy. It was never entirely clear what Cook meant by this even though he unveiled his intentions in a major speech in May 1997 that attempted to use the managerial and organisational language, that would become synonymous with 'New' Labour, to explain his 'ethical' approach. The speech was swiftly followed by the unveiling of a short film made by the film-maker, David Puttnam, designed to 'speak directly of our new goals and direction'.

Cook's stay at the Foreign Office was not a great success. His term was marked by British interventions in Kosovo and Sierra Leone, with the latter proving particularly controversial when allegations were made that a British company had supplied arms to supporters of the deposed president in contravention of a United Nations embargo. Cook was also embarrassed when his apparent offer to mediate in the dispute between India and Pakistan over Kashmir was rebuffed. In

2001, Cook was moved from the Foreign Office to be Leader of the House of Commons in what was widely seen as a demotion. He initially appeared to relish the prospect of reforming the practices and procedures of the Commons, however, and it was not until Britain became drawn into the moves to overthrow Saddam Hussein and his regime in Iraq that Cook decided to oppose openly the government of which he was a part.

By early 2003 Cook had become one of the key opponents in the government to the possibility of British military intervention in Iraq. On 17 March 2003 Cook resigned from the Cabinet at the height of what had become a crisis for Blair's government. His resignation statement set out the main reason for his departure: 'It is twenty years ago that I first joined Labour's Shadow Cabinet. It is with regret I have today resigned from its Cabinet. I can't accept collective responsibility for the decision to commit Britain now to military action in Iraq without international agreement or domestic support.'

This was followed by the usual exchange of letters between outgoing minister and Prime Minister before Cook delivered his resignation speech in the House of Commons later that day at which the House gave a standing ovation. Cook said that he could not back a war that did not have international or domestic support, nor could he be persuaded that there was 'an urgent and compelling reason for this action in Iraq'. The BBC's political editor, Andrew Marr, called Cook's performance 'without doubt one of the most effective and brilliant resignation speeches in modern British politics'. Although the government went on to survive the subsequent vote (even though 139 Labour MPs voted against war), Cook's resignation turned the spotlight on the International Development Minister, Clare Short, who was also a major opponent of military action from within the Cabinet.

The issue was raised the following day during a briefing from the Prime Minister's Office on Iraq. Clare Short, while openly critical of the government, had decided to stay in the Cabinet, (she would not resign for another two months), and the question was raised as to the extent that Short remained bound by the principle of collective cabinet responsibility. The response to this was 'yes', Short did, indeed, remain bound by the principle. When journalists pressed the point about the extent to which Short could continue 'agonising' while remaining a cabinet minister, the Prime Minister's spokesperson said it was 'still possible to have concerns'. In the case of Short, these much-expressed concerns were in relation to the reconstruction of Iraq and the broader Middle Eastern peace process.

The example of Clare Short is particularly revealing in terms of the current state of collective cabinet responsibility. As we have already shown, Short remained in the government for two months after she had first voiced her concerns in public over the prospect of war in Iraq, especially after the failure to secure a second United Nations resolution. Short made her first public breach of collective cabinet responsibility on Radio 4's 'Westminster Hour' on 9 March 2003. At some other time, Short would have been expected to resign or would have been sacked. In a letter to the *Daily Telegraph* on 11 March 2003, the Labour MP Graham Allen wrote: 'In permitting Clare Short to keep her Cabinet job, the Prime Minister has shown a willingness to put aside the longstanding convention regarding collective responsibility.'

As we are about to see, the debate surrounding the nature of prime ministerial power and the health of collective cabinet responsibility is a particularly lively one. Having eventually resigned in May 2003, Short touched upon the subject of collective cabinet responsibility in her resignation speech:

> In [Labour's] second term, the problem is the centralisation of power into the hands of the Prime Minister and an increasingly small number of advisers who make decisions in private without proper discussion. It is increasingly clear, I am afraid, that the Cabinet has become, in Bagehot's phrase, a dignified part of the constitution, it's gone the way of the Privy Council. There is no real collective responsibility because there is no collective; just diktats in favour of increasingly badly thought-through policy initiatives that come from on high.

Following the end of the war, the former Cabinet Secretary, Lord Butler, was asked by the government to conduct a review of the intelligence coverage available on programmes of weapons of mass destruction in Iraq. More significantly for us, he was also asked to make recommendations to the Prime Minister on the workings of the machinery of government, particularly the Cabinet.

Butler's overview of the government decision-making process had some significant points to make about the nature of collective ministerial decision making. For the political commentator, Peter Hennessey, Butler's criticisms on this specific issue were more fundamental than those criticisms directed at the intelligence community.[6] Butler concluded that:

- Government decision making was informal.
- Not enough use was made of established cabinet committee machinery.
- On the specific issue of intelligence relating to Iraq, the Cabinet Secretary was effectively removed from the 'chain' through which intelligence reaches the Prime Minister and that the Cabinet Secretariat was not part of various meetings on security and intelligence that would have helped cabinet ministers in 'discharging their collective responsibilities in defence and overseas policy matters'.
- Changes to two key posts in the Cabinet Secretariat (Defence and Europe) switched their roles to increase their responsibility to the Prime Minister rather than to the Cabinet as a whole.
- Cabinet had the opportunity to discuss Iraq in the year before the war. As war became more likely, however, smaller meetings of key ministers, civil servants and the military provided the framework for discussion and decision making in the government. Butler said: 'One inescapable consequence of this was to limit wider collective discussion and consideration by the Cabinet.'

Is cabinet government in decline?

It should become apparent from the discussion of collective cabinet responsibility that there are major questions on the status and 'health' of modern cabinet government. In this section we shall summarise the arguments for and against the suggestion that cabinet government is in decline.

Cabinet government is unwell

The evidence in support of this argument is starting to look fairly compelling. Cabinet meetings are now held only once a week, they are short (some lasting only twenty minutes according to one former minister), and are often nothing more than information-giving exercises or an opportunity to rubber-stamp decisions already taken. These developments, alongside Blair's leadership style, are often used to support the marginalisation theory of Cabinet and add to the general view that cabinet government is to all intent and purposes dead. As we shall see, the discussion on the health of cabinet government is closely linked to the debate on the 'presidentialism' of the Prime Minister and is something we shall cover in detail in the following chapter. The following points may all be used to support this argument that cabinet government is unwell:

- Shortened and less frequent cabinet meetings are increasingly used by the Prime Minister to gather the final collective seal of approval for decisions that are taken elsewhere. This particular approach to the Cabinet was clearly evident under Margaret Thatcher, and Blair has pushed the model further. The role of the modern Cabinet is therefore very restricted in terms of its traditional and expected role in the policy-making process.
- Power is increasingly centralised around the Prime Minister and a few senior ministers. The use of specialist advisers further marginalises the role of cabinet members. The increase in prime ministerial power has been augmented by the growing powers of the Prime Minister's Office that have allowed him or her more closely to oversee government strategy and monitor departmental work. It also allows the Prime Minister to initiate more policy from the center, with policy proposals passing backwards and forwards between Prime Minister's Office and departments in a way that increasingly cuts Cabinet out of the loop.
- Ministers may sometimes complain about the marginalisation of Cabinet, yet they do little themselves to promote genuine collegiality. According to this argument, ministers are interested only in their own departments. In this 'departmentalist' view of government the Cabinet becomes nothing more than the battleground on which struggles with the Treasury and other departments take place. This attitude adds to the general concerns about the health of the Cabinet.
- The modern media now focus largely on the Prime Minister as the key individual in the political system. In response, the Prime Minister must always be giving the impression of party control,

government leadership, and clear strategic and political vision combined with personal charisma and television 'presence'. It is the demands of a twenty-four-hour news media that have caused modern prime ministers to focus increasingly on the presentation of policy through the increasingly significant roles of press officers and 'spin doctors'. This concentration on the packaging and presentation of policy is particularly associated with the premiership of Tony Blair. A great deal of the modern packaging of British politics has been carried out at the expense of old-fashioned and traditional cabinet government.

- Continued membership of the European Union has a major impact on top-level decision making in such a way as to have strengthened the power of the Prime Minister while weakening the Cabinet. As the leading British negotiator in EU treaty making, the Prime Minister must be given considerable freedom to make deals in Britain's interests. Also, when other ministers are involved in policy making in the European Union, it is the Prime Minister who usually consents to any negotiating positions. Chairing important international meetings, such as the G8 summit in Scotland (July 2005), also greatly enhances the position of the Prime Minister, mostly at the expense of the Cabinet.

- As we have already seen, the application of the doctrine of collective responsibility has changed significantly in recent years, with a wider application applied in a much less stringent manner. This, taken with the other developments listed above, all point to a substantial collection of arguments that suggest cabinet government is not particularly healthy.

Cabinet government: alive and well

The first point to make about the modern Cabinet is that it is in a state of change and transition. Those arguments that seek to illustrate the 'decline' of cabinet government tend to base their analyses on a strict and unbending application of nineteenth-century conventions and agreements that overlooks the wholesale changes to government and policy making in the twentieth century. It is therefore not unreasonable to acknowledge that government by Cabinet is different now from the way it would have been in 1906. This is not automatically to assume, however, that the basic principles of cabinet government are on the critical list.

Mark Rathbone has put forward some key arguments in defence of the well-being of cabinet government.[7]

- **Taking major policy decisions without bringing them to Cabinet is nothing new** – Gladstone's conversion to Home Rule for Ireland was a personal decision about a major political issue and one that was thought through and introduced largely in isolation of any members of his Cabinet. Clement Attlee (Prime Minister 1945–51) quickly developed a style of managing the Cabinet that discouraged detailed discussions and stifled any dissenting voices. Rathbone quotes Kavanagh and Seldon's observation that 'every Prime Minister from Gladstone onwards has been accused of being 'dictatorial' or 'presidential'.

- **Short cabinet meetings do not necessarily mean the Prime Minister is ignoring the views of ministers** – long, detailed and regular cabinet meetings, which involve more than twenty ministers and various officials, may not really be the most efficient way of conducting government business. It is difficult to imagine Blair allowing the two-day cabinet meetings, which occasionally happened under Labour governments in the 1960s, to disrupt the flow of government business.

- **Is it really so surprising that prime ministers do not like being defeated in cabinet meetings?** – Given the leaks and rumours we have already discussed, it is difficult to imagine a prime minister suffering a defeat in Cabinet and for that defeat to remain a secret. Even if confidentiality was maintained, it is difficult to see how that prime minister could continue to head the government following a humiliating defeat by his or her colleagues. Prime ministers are therefore unlikely to bring any policy to Cabinet unless they are sure that their ministers will support it. In doing so, a prime minister will have assessed likely opposition and modified any aspects of the policy that may attract criticism. As Rathbone points out, this does not mean that the Cabinet does not have any power, merely that the constraints exercised by Cabinet tend to be informal.

- **Less frequent meetings of the full Cabinet do not mean the institution is in terminal decline** – viewing Cabinet in this way is to cast too narrow a focus on the issue. Cabinet committees now make up the greater part of the work of the cabinet system. It has been accepted for many years that decisions of cabinet committees have the full authority of cabinet decisions. Some critics of the system have seen cabinet committees as a means of increasing prime ministerial power; it is also true that terms of reference and membership of cabinet committees are decided by the Prime Minister. There are also examples of prime ministers, however, who have sought to use cabinet committees to avoid discussion and to steamroller their own policies through, but paying a high price for doing so. Rathbone uses Thatcher's cavalier treatment of Cabinet in the 1980s, and the high-profile resignations of senior ministers, as setting up the circumstances of her own downfall when, in 1990, she looked to her Cabinet for support against a leadership challenge and the support was not forthcoming.

- **Cabinet committees do not just bypass Cabinet, they are a means of managing it effectively** – if an issue is discussed at length by the most appropriate cabinet committee and its decision is merely reported to a full cabinet meeting, this is not necessarily an indication that cabinet government is in decline, it is more a sign that the Cabinet is functioning effectively. Critics of Blair's style of government have accused him of ignoring formal cabinet committees and choosing instead to hold 'bilateral' meetings on a one-to-one basis with individual ministers in order to arrive at a decision and there by to bypass wider discussion. Under Blair, however, the number of cabinet committees has risen considerably since 1997. Bilateral meetings may take place but this does not mean that cabinet committees are undermined.

George Jones of the London School of Economics has written extensively on the subject of the Prime Minister and the Cabinet. He encourages observers to avoid thinking of the Cabinet in its narrow sense. To do so, he argues, makes the Cabinet appear a very limited body. Far better, he writes, to think of the Cabinet as a complete system that has at its heart the senior ministers of the Cabinet around which all the other elements of cabinet government revolve. These satellites of the central Cabinet include the cabinet committees, the Cabinet Office and the Cabinet Secretary, all the various units that now make up the Prime Minister's Office together senior government members of all government departments and the Treasury. This view will be discussed in more detail in Chapter 9 when we outline the theory of a 'core executive'.

Concluding points

In his biography of Blair, Rentoul referred to the 'new low' in the history of cabinet government. Brief meetings, decisions taken elsewhere, business conducted in cabinet committees and the increased use of bilaterals all point to a style that is 'hub and spoke rather than collegiate'.[8] Mo Mowlam was also highly critical of Blair's style, especially the 'centralising tendency and arrogance of No.10'.[9]

It would appear that cabinet government in its current manifestation is not functioning entirely in accordance with the classic and traditional understanding of its role in government. The extent to which this situation is terminal, however, is less clear. Rathbone uses a famous *Monty Python* sketch to illustrate the potential that still remains in the cabinet system of government as its supporters wish to view it. For much of the 1980s, argues Rathbone, cabinet government appeared to be dead but, in reality, it was just stunned and, in the end, awoke to give its owner a savage pecking. Whether cabinet government will ever reassert itself completely is another matter. For better or worse, we now have a system of government focused largely on the Prime Minister. The Cabinet may on occasions have the opportunity to exert itself over the Prime Minister in brief and dramatic shows of 'pecking' yet, between these times, it is difficult to imagine a return to a genuinely collegiate cabinet style of government that may never have existed anyway.

••

 What you should have learnt from reading this chapter

At the start of this chapter we discussed the definitions and traditional views of how the doctrine of collective responsibility came into being and how it is supposed to work. We then went on to examine the doctrine of collective cabinet responsibility by looking at recent events and the impact of these events, especially those surrounding the war in Iraq, on the condition of cabinet government. The discussion in this chapter was concluded by an overview of the debate on the 'health' of cabinet government: is cabinet government 'unwell' or are reports of its death exaggerated? There are strong arguments for both sides of the debate. It is certainly the case that the leadership styles of recent prime ministers may be interpreted as a marginalisation of Cabinet, and the very vocal denunciations of recent ex-ministers support this view. Alternatively there are arguments that suggest modern cabinet government is 'different' owing to the changing wider political context but this is not to say it is incapable of reasserting itself at some point in the future.

Glossary of key terms

Agreement to differ This is where the doctrine of collective cabinet responsibility is relaxed to allow cabinet ministers to disagree in public on a specific issue.

Collective cabinet responsibility The doctrine stating that all members of the government are collectively responsible for its decisions. In recent years it has been suggested that the application of the doctrine has undergone considerable change.

Confidence Government will remain in power only for as long as it retains the confidence of the House of Commons. Confidence is always assumed unless a confidence vote is lost by the government.

Confidentiality Discussion in Cabinet must be confidential if open and frank exchanges of views are to take place. Unanimity may be a 'fiction' but confidentiality must be maintained.

Free votes When cabinet ministers are freed from the requirement to vote with the government. Usually on moral or controversial social issues such as the death penalty or abortion.

Leaks When information confidential to Cabinet finds its way into the public domain.

Unanimity All members of the government speak and vote together in Parliament – unless an exception is made. The universal application of unanimity may well be a 'constitutional fiction'.

Likely examination questions

Short questions

Describe what is meant by the term 'collective cabinet responsibility'.

Briefly describe those occasions when collective responsibility has been breached.

Explain why events in Iraq have had a major impact on the doctrine of collective responsibility.

Describe the key functions of the Cabinet.

Briefly summarise the arguments that can be used to support the claim that 'cabinet government is in decline'.

Briefly summarise the arguments that can be used to support the claim that 'cabinet government is alive and well'.

Essay questions

'The Cabinet is dead.' Discuss.

The doctrine of collective cabinet responsibility no longer exists. To what extent do you agree?

To what extent would you agree with the suggestion that smaller cabinets function better than larger cabinets.

How far have the Blair governments since 1997 contributed to the downgrading of Cabinet?

Revision task

Research and produce a revision table of two columns. Label one 'Cabinet government is dead' and label the other 'Cabinet government is alive'. Use bullet points to list key pieces of evidence in each column.

 ## Helpful websites

www.number10.gov.uk/

www.direct.gov.uk/

www.cabinetoffice.gov.uk/

www.civilservice.gov.uk

 ## Suggestions for further reading

Allen, G. (2001) *The Last Prime Minister* (Politico's).

Benn, T. (1981) *Arguments for Democracy* (Penguin).

Burch, M. and Halliday, I. (1996) *The British Cabinet System* (Prentice Hall).

Dorey, P. (1991) 'Cabinet Committees', *Talking Politics*, vol. 4.1, autumn 1991.

Ellis, D. (1980) 'Collective Ministerial Responsibility and Collective Solidarity', *Public Law*, 367.

Gay, O. and Powell, T. (2004) 'The Collective Responsibility of Ministers' (House of Commons Research Paper, Nov. 2004, 04/82).

Hennessy, P. (2002) 'The Blair Government in Historical Perspective', *History Today*, Jan. 2002.

Hennessy, P. (2004) 'Systems Failure at Heart of Government', *Independent*, 16 July 2004.

Jones, B (ed.) (2004) *Politics UK*, 5th edn (Longman Pearson), chapter 19.

Kavanagh, D. and Seldon, A. (1999) *The Powers behind the Prime Minister* (HarperCollins).

Magee, E. and Garnett, M. (2002) 'Is Cabinet Government Dead?', *Politics Review*, vol. 12.1, Sep. 2002.

Mowlam, M. (2002) *Momentum: The Struggle for Peace, Politics and the People* (Hodder).

Rathbone, M. (2003) 'The British Cabinet', *Talking Politics*, vol. 16.1, Sep. 2003.

Rentoul, J. (2001) *Tony Blair: Prime Minister* (Time Warner).

Sampson, A. (2004) *Who Runs This Place? The Anatomy of Britain in the 21st Century* (Murray) chapter 7.

Thomas, G. (2002) 'The Prime Minister and Cabinet', *Politics Review*, vol. 11.4, 2002.

CHAPTER 5

The Prime Minister: Power

Contents

Overview

The focus here will be on the Prime Minister and prime ministerial power. In May 2005 Tony Blair became the first Labour Prime Minister to win three consecutive elections. Like Margaret Thatcher, the Prime Minister who dominated the last years of the twentieth century, Blair has done much to provoke major appraisals of what it now means to be Prime Minister of Britain. The roles and powers of the office have been the subject of much debate. This chapter will examine these key areas and point the way to the next section of the book that will deal with the bureaucracy and support systems available to the Prime Minister.

Key issues to be covered in this chapter

- The role and powers of the modern Prime Minister
- The internal and external constraints on the powers of the Prime Minister

Introduction

Since 1979 only three individuals have held the office of Prime Minister. Even by the relatively stable standards of western liberal democracies, this is a remarkable achievement. This focus of power in the hands and personalities of a small élite says much about the nature of the office of Prime Minister and the political system that upholds and maintains the position. For the larger part of the period since 1979, two individuals – Margaret Thatcher and Tony Blair – who between them illustrate significant factors relating to the modern position of the chief executive, have held the position of Prime Minister. In looking at these two individuals, there are also major points to be made in terms of key differences and, perhaps more interestingly, key similarities. Moreover, since the events surrounding the war in Iraq from 2003 onwards, there has been in Britain a heightened sense of a debate relating to prime ministerial power.

Origins and history

As we have already explained, the origins of the office of Prime Minister may be traced back to the Glorious Revolution of 1688 and the development of cabinet government during the reign of William III and the subsequent reign of the Hanoverian kings, George I, II, and III.

It is generally agreed that Sir Robert Walpole was the first person to hold the office that we now recognise as 'Prime Minister'. Although George III would wrestle back some of the powers of the monarch from the Prime Minister, the essential functions of the office had been established. The British political system may have undergone substantial change between Walpole and Blair, but the fundamental prime ministerial characteristics remain. The Prime Minister:

- May exercise prerogative powers delegated by the monarch.
- Will largely determine the composition of the Cabinet.
- Will be expected to maintain and lead a unified Cabinet capable of presenting a coherent programme and confident face to Parliament.
- Must command the support of the majority of Parliament – especially the House of Commons.

- Must be able to display sufficient political authority and ability to become chief policy maker across the whole range of government business.

It is difficult to imagine a situation now where a Prime Minister could be a distant and largely unknown figure but it is worth pointing out that Robert Peel was probably the first modern holder of the office to have a personal profile and recognition that went beyond the enclosed world of Parliament and party. This widespread public recognition of the Prime Minister took further leaps with the two great titans of nineteenth-century politics, Gladstone and Disraeli, and continued through to the twentieth-century in the shape of Salisbury, Asquith and Lloyd George. In this sense, the personalised nature of the office, which has reached the almost forensic personal scrutiny of the likes of Thatcher and Blair, is merely the product of long-term historical trends in the evolution of the post. Having looked at the origins and history of the Prime Minister, we may discuss the position in terms of roles and powers. The following text box will be useful in setting out in detail the discussion we are about to have.

The role of the Prime Minister

The development of the modern Prime Minister and the modern relationship between Prime Minister and Cabinet is due primarily to the work of the Liberal Prime Minister David Lloyd George and a senior civil servant, Maurice Hankey.

The reforms introduced by Lloyd George and Hankey are essentially those that govern the organisation of the British Cabinet today. They are summarised in the table below.

There is one other aspect of the 1916 reforms that has been developed and refined by subsequent premiers. In order to meet on a more informal basis with specialist advisers and civil servants, Lloyd George took over one of the garden sheds at the rear of 10 Downing Street and established a private secretariat – probably the first example of what we now refer to as kitchen cabinets – and specialist advisers, the type revealed by the Hutton Inquiry meeting with Blair in the Prime Minister's 'den' and taking key unminuted decisions while draped across sofas and easy chairs.

Box 5.1 Prime ministerial roles and powers: an overview

The roles and powers of the British Prime Minister are notoriously difficult to set down in a clear and unambiguous way. This text box will introduce you to some of the key concepts, themes and distinctions in the order that we shall cover them in the following pages:

Role of the Prime Minister
When we refer to the 'role' of the Prime Minister, we refer to the 'parts' that the Prime Minister plays as if he or she were an actor in a film. The roles we will discuss here include: leader of government, leader of foreign policy, leader of a political party and communicator-in-chief. We will also see how the Prime Minister is also required to play two roles in the same film, as it were, as **head of state** and **head of government**. You may wish to look again at chapter 1 to remind yourself of these particular distinctions.

Powers of the Prime Minister
The powers of the Prime Minister are the visible and legitimate means by which he or she is able to play the role. This is strongly linked to the idea of Prime ministerial **authority** which is where the powers actually come from and that are accepted as being **legitimate** sources of power. We will refer to the powers of the Prime Minister as being **constitutional/formal** and **informal/fluid**.

Constitutional/formal powers
Those powers that were historically performed by the monarch and are known as **prerogative** powers. We will look at these powers of the Prime Minister as **head of state and head of government**.

Informal/fluid powers
As the phrase suggests, these are much more **flexible** powers and the way in which they are exercised reflects greatly on the style and leadership of the Prime Minister. The powers here are mostly those linked with government and include the political leadership of a party, speaking on behalf of the government and determining government policy.

The constitutional position of the Prime Minister is unclear. To put it bluntly, there is no constitutional definition of a Prime Minister's role. Looking at statutes does little to clarify the issue as there are no statutory references to the office of Prime Minister before

Table 5.1 Cabinet government: the 1916 reforms

Before	After
Cabinet meetings and decisions were not minuted or circulated.	Minutes were taken of discussions and decisions. These minutes were circulated to other main areas of government.
Cabinet was attempting to deal with all policy issues. The increased workload meant that Cabinet was not always able to give specialised areas of policy due consideration.	A cabinet committee system was established that would consider the specialised areas of policy and report back to the full Cabinet with specific recommendations. Ministers from outside the Cabinet sat on these sub-committees and allowed those with specialist knowledge to contribute to the policy-making process. Lloyd George chaired the more important cabinet committees.
The Cabinet had no specific bureaucracy to organise and structure its work.	Hankey became the first holder of the office of Cabinet Secretary. Hankey therefore became the most senior civil servant in Whitehall and helped organise cabinet business and maintain cabinet unity. A Cabinet Secretariat was also established. This was headed by the Cabinet Secretary and was charged with ensuring that all parts of government understood and worked towards achieving all Cabinet decisions.

1937. Nevertheless, the role and powers of the Prime Minister are now central to the workings of the entire British system of government, and it is to these considerations that we shall now turn. We shall look first at the different roles of the Prime Minister and then go on to discuss the powers available to the Prime Minister to execute his or her various roles.

Leadership of government

In terms of the origins of the office, this is the key role and official function of the British Prime Minister. It is the central aspect of everything else the Prime Minister does. In this role, the Prime Minister is effectively the head of the executive and is in charge of controlling the Cabinet, overseeing the Civil Service and government agencies, and will be ultimately answerable for all the decisions the government makes.

In leading the government the Prime Minister must control the Cabinet. When a Prime Minister fails to control the Cabinet then it is unlikely that he or she will be an effective leader of government. In these situations the Prime Minister will probably be replaced, either by an electorate that recognises the weakness of their position or by their own party which will remove him or her from power and choose a replacement.

As head of the executive, the Prime Minister is also the head of government policy. Most policy in modern government is a product of departments and party policy-making machinery, yet the Prime Minister retains a key influence over the election manifesto and the annual Queen's Speech outlining the legislative programme of the government for the new parliamentary session. It is at this point that the Prime Minister may choose to highlight certain policies as central to the aims of the government in the coming months. A good example of this may be seen in the 2005 Queen's Speech where the notion of 'respect' was singled out as a crucial factor in the direction of government policy in the third Labour term. Street crime, attendance at school, even the 'hoodies' menace were emphasised to the media as being central to what the government saw as its key priorities. Tony Blair was happy to push this agenda as a response to the decline in Labour support during the 2005 election and as a means of diverting attention from himself and issues of trust as dominant political issues.

Leadership of foreign policy

The Prime Minister is now the senior representative of the United Kingdom overseas. Prime Ministers represent the United Kingdom at meetings of the United Nations, the G8 group, European Councils (in a heightened role when the Britain has the Chair of the European Union, as it had most recently from June to December 2005) and in the twice-yearly meetings of the Commonwealth heads of government. Alongside these examples of regular and structured meetings, modern Prime Ministers have found themselves increasingly called upon to react and formulate policy to wider world events. All three recent Prime Ministers have committed British forces to armed conflicts, and all of them spent varying amounts of time and enthusiasm on seeking to achieve broad agreement to peace proposals in Northern Ireland.

Foreign policy may prove to be the key motif of Blair's time as Prime Minister. In his time in office, Blair has committed British forces to five wars in the space of six years, the most controversial, and potentially the most politically damaging, being British involvement in the war to remove Saddam Hussein from power in Iraq. This, according to John Kampfner, is 'some feat' especially for a man who came to office in 1997 'knowing precious little about foreign affairs'.[1]

Leadership of a political party
The Prime Minister is now always leader of the majority party in the House of Commons. As such, he or she is the principal figure in the business of the House of Commons, especially during the weekly gladiatorial conquest known as question time. Performances during these thirty-minute sessions are now analysed and picked over in a similar way to reviews and reports of the performances of actors or singers on stage. This has become particularly emphasised since the televising of Commons business in 1989, although the instant analysis of question time on the BBC's Radio 5 Live is closer to the judging on *Pop Idol* than it is to sober analysis of the issues that have just been debated.

As leader of a political party, the Prime Minister must also ensure that the party is disciplined and organised enough to win elections and retain power. In this role, the Prime Minister also represents the public face of the party of which he or she is leader. In elections, the voters will be less likely to see the Prime Minister as somehow separate from the party as they might do in a presidential-type election. Blair's personal unpopularity must therefore be seen as a key factor in the substantial reduction in the Labour vote during the 2005 general election. His role as Prime Minister did little to save him from the wrath of voters who turned away from the Labour Party as a protest around issues relating to his 'trust'.

Communicator-in-chief

> BBC REPORTER. Would you like to explain Labour's plans for the election campaign?
>
> CLEMENT ATTLEE. No.

This 1955 exchange between Prime Minister and a BBC reporter illustrates the medieval period of political television. It is now an essential requirement that the holder of the post of Prime Minister be an expert communicator and polished media performer. In an era of twenty-four hour rolling news channels, of televised Parliament and the instant political fix of the world wide web the Prime Minister must be comfortable in front of the camera, be ready to joust with the likes of Jeremy Paxman and John Humphrys, and be ready to respond to national and international events with little time for preparation. He or she must gauge the public mood exactly.

Recent Prime Ministers have performed the role of communicator-in-chief in various ways. At the height of her powers, Margaret Thatcher could be forceful and magisterial, and was frequently capable of overpowering her interlocutors by the sheer force of her personality. She also developed a particularly effective combination of incredulity and outrage when it became clear to her that someone was in the process of daring to disagree. It is noticeable on occasions that Blair gives signs of a similar sense of dismay as he leans forward, open palmed, and explains something for what seems like the tenth time to people who really should be paying more attention. In a deliberate move to offer a different style form that of his predecessor, John Major adopted a much more conciliatory mood in his style of communication. The hectoring 'I knew I was right all along' approach of Thatcher was replaced by a more mild and gentle tone of forced familiarity. Of the three, Tony Blair is probably the most accomplished political communicator. While his clashes in the Commons lack some of the punch and sheer enjoyment of the Thatcher era, he showed himself to be an adept manipulator of political communication during his first term of office. His response to the death of the Princess of Wales appeared to capture perfectly the extraordinary mood of mourning and grief that characterised the following week. Similarly, in the immediate aftermath of the London bombings of July 2005, he was able to tap into the national mood using the appropriate tone even though, in the words of one of his biographers, it is little more than an ability to 'pick up and reflect back the banality of majority'.[2]

The powers of the Prime Minister

Having established the key roles of the Prime Minister, we can now move on to discuss the sources of power and authority that give him or her the means by which the various roles may be exercised.

Authority of the Prime Minister

If the Prime Minister is legitimately to use the powers we are about to discuss, it is necessary for the holder of the office to be able to claim to have the authority to do so. Prime ministerial authority is best summed up in the four-part table below:

Case study: prime ministerial authority

In 1990 the Conservative Party in Parliament voted to remove Margaret Thatcher from power and quickly chose John Major to replace her as leader of the party. Major therefore became Prime Minister having been elected only as leader of the Conservative Party by Conservative MPs. There was no general election. Thatcher had clearly lost the support of her party – both within and outside of Parliament – and with that loss of support there was the accompanying loss of authority. There were also clear indicators in 1990 that Thatcher had lost the popular support from the people that she had most appealed to throughout most of the mid-1980s, and she could therefore not claim to have the authority derived from three of the four sources listed in the table above.

In 2005 questions are being asked about the nature of Tony Blair's authority. With a much reduced parliamentary majority on top of a public announcement that he has fought his last election as leader, and with voters expressing major doubts on the issue of his personal integrity, it could be argued that Blair is dangerously close to losing the same three bases of power that Thatcher lost in 1990 and which caused her downfall.

The powers we are about to discuss are substantial, as are the bases of authority on which those powers are constructed. It is always worth

Table 5.2 Sources of prime ministerial authority

Crown	Parliament
• The Prime Minister is appointed by the monarch who asks him/her to form a government after a general election. • The process may be largely ceremonial, but does confer some legitimacy on the outcome of the election and the position of the Prime Minister.	• The largest party in Parliament, of which the Prime Minister is usually the leader, confers authority on this person. • Irrespective of the other powers the Prime Minister may enjoy, if the holder of the office loses the respect and goodwill of his or her party in Parliament, then authority is lost at the same time and he or she will be remove from office by the party.

People	Party
• Voters appear to see general elections increasingly as contest between leaders. • Prime Ministers may use the doctrine of mandate to declare they have the authority of the people to govern. • Recent election results – especially in 2005 – have caused some commentators to question how valid the notion of 'authority from the people' is when based on such a small proportion of the population.	• The Prime Minister is almost always the leader of the largest party in Parliament. • To secure the leadership of his or her party and to then go on to win a general election and be offered the position of Prime Minister requires the continued blessing of authority from the party.

noting, however, how the four-square model of authority may shift significantly to the point where all the powers of the Prime Minister, either constitutional or evolutionary, can do little to save him or her from being removed from office.

We have already made the case that the position of the British Prime Minister is not clearly stated in any written parts of the Constitution. The office has evolved in such a way, however, that we may refer to certain powers of the Prime Minister as being constitutional in that they are essentially permanent, have a status almost equivalent to the formal laws of the United Kingdom and have been exercised by Prime Ministers for more than 300 years.

Balanced alongside these constitutional powers are those powers that a Prime Minister may enjoy at any particular point in history given the particular circumstances and events associated with his or her period in office. These evolving or 'fluid' powers may be decided by the difference between peace and war and the differences between periods of economic growth and recession. These powers may also owe much to the nature of the government that the Prime Minister leads. The evolving/fluid powers of Tony Blair, for instance, may be fewer now, in the aftermath of the 2005 general election, than they were in 1997 following the first Labour victory under his leadership. Finally, this second set of powers may be very closely linked to the personality and style of individual leaders. The direct and often confrontational use of these evolving powers as used by Margaret Thatcher, for instance, contrasted markedly with the more conciliatory approach of John Major.

Constitutional powers

Often referred to by writers as the 'formal' powers of the Prime Minister, the key to these powers is contained in those functions historically performed by the monarch and known as prerogative powers. These prerogative powers fall into two separate categories:

- those where the Prime Minister acts on behalf of the monarch as the head of state;
- those that are carried out as head of government.

Because, as we have already stated, the distinction between 'state' and 'government' is notoriously blurred in the United Kingdom, the two formal constitutional roles of the Prime Minister are equally confused. It is often pointed out that only in the United States is a similar dual role accepted though, in America, it is usually made clear by the President in which capacity he is acting. The British Prime Minister is rarely as helpful. The following chart, adapted from McNaughton,

Table 5.3 The formal constitutional powers of the Prime Minister

As head of state	As head of government
Military and intelligence powers – the Prime Minister is in charge of the overall conduct of the armed forces and controls all branches and operations of the intelligence services.	**Chair of Cabinet** – here, the Prime Minister acts as chief executive in the key committee of the government.
Foreign Treaty powers – the Prime Minister negotiates all foreign treaties with other powers and with international organisations such as the United Nations, NATO and the European Union.	**Hiring and firing** – it is important to note that this power of patronage is exclusively in the of the Prime Minister and has expanded to the point where it covers something approaching 150 government posts.
Control of the Civil Service – although the administrative control of the Civil Service is in the hands of the Cabinet Secretary, it is the Prime Minister who shoulders the responsibility for the overall conduct and organisation of the UK bureaucracy and who has a major say in the appointment of senior civil servants.	**Dissolving Parliament** – a significant power, one that is not always available in presidential systems. The Prime Minister decides when Parliament is to be dissolved in order to call a general election at any point before the full five-year period when an election would have to be held.
Senior appointments – covers senior judges and archbishops /bishops of the Church of England. In this function the Prime Minister is called upon formally to approve suggestions put forward by the Lord Chancellor's Department and the Archbishop of Canterbury.	**Senior appointments of public bodies** – not the same power as the one opposite and should not be confused with it. The bodies here are typically public bodies or quangos, such as the Arts Council or the BBC. The Prime Minister may also be called upon to make appointments to some university posts.

attempts to summarise the formal constitutional powers of the Prime Minister in both roles.[3]

To the powers and roles listed above we could add that the Prime Minister is also the leader of a national political party and must also lead and represent that party in Parliament. It is also essential that modern Prime Ministers develop the role and necessary skills of chief government communicator, never missing the opportunity to defend and represent the work of the government. In recent years, commentators such as Foley have noted how Prime Ministers have increasingly come to personify the actions of their government, especially in their dealings with, and handling of, the media.[4]

Informal and fluid powers

Broadly speaking, the informal and fluid powers of the Prime Minister are associated mostly with his or her role as the leader of the political party in power. The powers are best described as informal and fluid for two main reasons:

- the Constitution is equally as vague on this set of powers as it is on the more formal powers, and they are likely to change and evolve over time and in response to any particular set of circumstances – hence the use of the phrase 'fluidity';
- the informal/fluid powers are very much a reflection of the ways in which they are used by specific Prime Ministers.

There are three key informal powers. They have already been outlined at various points in this chapter, and a brief summary of them will suffice at this point:

- *Leader of the majority parliamentary party* – without the support and continued goodwill of his or her party, it is difficult for a Prime Minister to claim the greater political authority of governing the country.
- *Chief spokesperson for the government* – these powers are exercised mainly in the Commons during question time, and outside Parliament as the main focus of media attention. The party in power will look to the Prime Minister to give the best impression of party policy, in the Commons and to the mass media.
- *Head policy-maker for the government* – this particular power is very much an index of individual prime ministerial style and power

and will reveal much about the particular ways in which a Prime Minister chooses to manage the Cabinet.

Are the powers of the Prime Minister increasing?

The larger debate on this question will take place in the following chapters. For now, we will satisfy ourselves with giving a brief overview of the key arguments surrounding the nature of prime ministerial power in the early twenty-first century.

Richard Crossman and Tony Benn, two former cabinet ministers in Labour governments, have argued variously that the powers of the British Prime Minister have increased, particularly at the expense of the Cabinet. In more recent studies, writers such as Foley and Johnson[5] have commented extensively on the powers of the British Prime Minister, especially in terms of what they perceive to be the increasingly 'presidential' nature of prime ministerial power. This is not to say that everyone necessarily agrees with these arguments. Jones and Burch, both writing in the late 1980s and early 1990s, have advised caution when comparing Prime Ministers with Presidents, making the point that a Prime Minister is only as powerful as his or her colleagues allow him or her to be.[6] The fall from power of Margaret Thatcher, and the possibility of a slow re-emergence of something approaching cabinet government following the May 2005 general election, suggest that, while the Prime Minister undoubtedly has substantial powers and that those powers have indeed grown in recent decades, it may not be entirely accurate to refer to a 'British presidency' in a way that implies a direct comparison with the American system.

Checks on prime ministerial power

However much one may make the case for the impressive collection of powers available to the Prime Minister, it is important to balance this against a collection of significant constraints. We may summarise these constraints as being 'internal' and 'external'.

Internal constraints

Internal constraints focus almost exclusively on the nature of the relationship between the Prime Minister and the Cabinet, and invariably include some discussion on prime ministerial style and personality. No matter how 'strong' a Prime Minister may be, he or she is in a difficult position if a majority in the Cabinet is determined to oppose a major issue. Prime Ministers may attempt to subvert these revolts by attempting to keep issues off the cabinet agenda. Margaret Thatcher's decisions regarding American attacks on Libya, for instance, were taken independently of Cabinet and there were no cabinet discussions. It may be possible for a Prime Minister to act in this way over a relatively isolated incident, such as the bombing of a country in North Africa by a third party, but it is rather more difficult to prevent crucial and long-term domestic issues, such as health, education or the economy, from appearing on the cabinet agenda for too long.

Cabinet may defy the Prime Minister. Thatcher faced several climb-downs in the early 1980s and was almost certainly restrained from pushing ahead with some of her more radical industrial relations and privatisation plans by more circumspect members of her Cabinet. It is also highly likely that the decision to join the European Exchange Rate Mechanism in October 1990 was more to do with pressure from a determined majority in Cabinet rather than with any great enthusiasm from Thatcher herself. Other examples of this type of constraint include Thatcher's defeat in Cabinet over the proposed sale of Land Rover to General Motors, and John Major's reluctant acceptance of the second round of VAT on domestic energy supplies in the budget of 1994 (a measure defeated in the Commons later that year).

In reality, Prime Ministers do not bring to Cabinet any of their policies unless they have already ensured that they will be endorsed by ministers. This leads to the situation that constraints exercised by Cabinet are largely informal. It may also be the case that Blair is the most effective manager of the cabinet agenda as well. Rentoul quotes Peter Hennessey who has written that the usual agenda for cabinet meetings was:

> stunningly unrevealing . . . consisting only of three regular items, Next Week's Business in Parliament, Domestic and Economic Affairs, and Foreign Affairs (for the first two years there was a fourth, 'Europe' which was subsumed in the second and third items from mid-1999) and an attachment known in New Labour language as The Grid – a plan drawn up by the Strategic Communications Unit of events and ministerial announcements for the coming week.[7]

External constraints

The external influences the internal. While the Prime Minister may go to considerable lengths to control the nature of his or her relationship with the Cabinet, there is little that can be done effectively to control external factors. These same factors may be as significant a constraint on prime ministerial power as anything that passes between chief executive and ministers around the cabinet table. Parliament is the first external constraint that we need to discuss before going on to look at party, public opinion and the media.

Parliament

The size of the majority in the Commons is the key factor in determining the effectiveness of Parliament as an external constraint. It was unlikely, for example, that any back-bench rebellion could have been successful during the high years of Thatcher's governments between 1983 and 1987 when the Conservatives had a majority of almost 150 seats. Similarly, Blair's 1997 majority of 179 and his 167 majority in 2001 were equally unlikely to result in any government defeat in the Commons. Compare those examples, however, with the Major government after 1992 with its small majority of twenty-one. Here, the likelihood of defeat from the back benches was much more real and is illustrated by his difficulties with the ratification of the Maastricht Treaty in 1994 which was settled only by his tactic in making Maastricht a vote of confidence, thus raising the issue of dissolution and election. The position of Blair in relation to Parliament after the 2005 election is interesting. The majority after 2005 no longer represents the largest infantry of any post-war Prime Minister yet does not recreate the tiny platoon behind Major after 1992. The make-up of that majority is very different from Blair's two previous governments, however. The fresh-faced 'new' Labour intake of 1997 and 2001 has been largely dissipated. What Blair feels behind his back after May 2005 is a much more traditional, much older and much more potentially hostile collection of backbenchers than he has previously had to deal with. It is unlikely, under the circumstances, that a back-bench revolt would be successful, yet it is interesting to ponder how 'close scrapes' from the previous administration – top-up fees in particular – would have been handled with such a small majority. We may therefore be entering a period when the potential constraint of Parliament is greater than at any time since 1992.

On the whole, however, provided they do not lead a minority or weak coalition government, Prime Ministers need not become unduly concerned about the nature of parliamentary constraints. Blair may well be subjected to a slightly rougher ride at Prime Minister's question time than used to be the case, and a larger and partially revitalised opposition under a new leader may seek to 'damage' the Prime Minister, yet it is highly unlikely that any mortal blow will be struck. One final point to note in this discussion on Parliament, and one that we unfortunately do not have enough space to go into in greater detail, is the potential constraint that may be exercised by the House of Lords. We tend to focus our analysis on the Commons alone and, in doing so, forget that, for Thatcher and for Blair, irrespective of their huge Commons majorities, it has often been the upper chamber that has been able to provide the government with its sternest opposition and obstruction. We must now turn to the second external constraint: the party.

Party

The fact that the Prime Minister is also the leader of a political party is often overlooked. Blair, in particular, has been less than enthusiastic about portraying himself as a purely 'party' leader and, as a consequence, his relationship with the party is often strained. In this respect, his position is similar to that of Margaret Thatcher: a powerful Prime Minister capable of delivering large parliamentary majorities yet, in many ways, an outsider in, and often at odds with, their own party.

At the time of writing (summer 2005), the Conservative Party is currently reviewing the means by which it chooses its leader; the system in the Labour Party is unlikely to change. In short, both leaders are elected by a larger constituency than used to be the case, and they must therefore show sensitivity to this fact. The prime ministerial use of patronage, already discussed elsewhere, is a key factor here. Factions or groups in the party must be seen to be acknowledged in ministerial appointments, as should the rewards to party 'favourites' or those with party power bases – John Prescott is a good example here. We must be careful not to overstate the case however.

The modernising project of 'New' Labour has substantially eroded the power of the constituencies and the trade unions. The National Executive Committee of Labour, essentially its elected leadership group, is no longer the power in the party it once was. The annual conference once offered highly entertaining opportunities for the ritual 'calling to account' of the party leadership and cabinet ministers (when in government) but such opportunities are no more.

The Conservatives have never had to contend with a genuine mass membership organised along democratic lines and laying any kind of claim to an input into the policy-making process of the party. Even recent attempts by William Hague to introduce internal party democracy have not been a huge success and may even have been responsible for encouraging the leadership to push its policies increasingly to the right, something the electorate as a whole appears not to have appreciated. Conservative leaders must also find ways of dealing with the influential 1922 Committee which is made up of all back-bench Conservative MPs. This group occasionally made life difficult for Margaret Thatcher and more so for John Major who found himself being challenged frequently over his European policies. Having made these points about the Conservatives, it is important to stress that the power in that party flows essentially from the top to the bottom. Ministerial teams, election strategies and manifestos are all determined by the leadership. The party may no longer give the impression of unity that it once did, and it certainly gets through leaders on a more regular basis than was once the case, but the constraints on the power of a Conservative Prime Minister from his or her party should not be overstated.

The power of the Prime Minister, then, is not to be underestimated when discussed in relation to the party membership. In office, a Prime Minister is usually able to call on much bigger battalions than those available to party members and, as long as the party continues to win elections (Thatcher being the obvious exception), the Prime Minister should be more than capable of dealing with any trouble or dissent from his or her wider party membership.

Public opinion
Public opinion, especially when expressed in terms of unpopularity, may exert constraints on the Prime Minister by framing the attitudes

of Cabinet and of Parliament. The best example of this is Margaret Thatcher. In 1990, when it appeared that Thatcher had lost public respect and that the Conservatives were in danger of losing the next election, the party moved quickly and ruthlessly to get rid of her, three general election victories in a row notwithstanding. In the 2005 general election, the popularity of Blair became an electoral issue. Public unease about his personal role in the run-up to the war in Iraq began to be seen and discussed as an issue of 'trust' and was certainly one of the key reasons for the slump in Labour Party support at the general election. This was a far cry from Blair's 90 per cent public-approval rating during the later part of 1997, a figure that could only enhance his standing and authority in the party, Cabinet and Parliament.

Public opinion and popularity may not be the most crucial constraints on the power of a Prime Minister but they should not be completely ignored either. The personal attacks and questions surrounding Blair's integrity in 2005 have resulted in a somewhat chastened and wiser Prime Minister desperate to focus the political agenda on domestic, rather than foreign, policy issues while plotting his exit strategy from the centre stage of British politics.

The media

The media are the means and the measurement of public opinion and popularity. According to Richard Rose, Blair is the third Prime Minister of what he refers to as the 'new style television generation' alongside Thatcher and Major. Now, more than ever, politics is a wholly televised aspect of public life and requires its practitioners to be polished and accomplished media performers. Again, the constraint here is less through the media directly but rather more through the impact of the media on the nature of the relationship between the Prime Minister and Cabinet. If a Prime Minister is ceaselessly attacked by the media, and is unable to handle these attacks effectively, then he or she is very likely to be weakened in his or her relations with the Cabinet.

Case study: Richard Rose and 'intermestic politics'

In his hugely readable and thought-provoking study *The Prime Minister in a Shrinking World*, Richard Rose examines the power of the British

Prime Minister from a slightly different perspective.[8] Rose argues that the powers and responsibilities of the Prime Minister are increasingly shaped and constrained by subsidiarity and by globalisation. According to Rose, some powers of the Prime Minister are being devolved downwards while, at the same time, other powers are being drawn upwards, outwards and even overseas. This is mainly due, Rose explains, to the speed at which globalisation has accelerated and the way in which economic, military and political decisions are often taken by a growing number of multinational intergovernmental and supranational bodies.

Rose goes on to argue that modern British Prime Ministers now find themselves in a strange situation. They may well command huge parliamentary majorities at Westminster yet, in an age of devolved assemblies and regional models based on the European Union, the Prime Minister may well find it difficult to exert political authority across the whole country. Here, Rose is restating an observation made by other commentators: the British constitution may well have evolved in such a way as to give the Prime Minister substantial powers but what it has not done is to bestow the kind of powers whereby he or she can be certain that prime ministerial plans and policies are turned into actions that actually achieve anything. This leads to Prime Ministers becoming increasingly occupied with the co-ordination of strategy and political management rather than concentrating on policy development. At this point, Rose is able to make the distinction between what he refers to as the 'old school' of Prime Ministers from Churchill through to Attlee and the new-style 'television generation' of Thatcher, Major and Blair. Sandwiched between these two groups are what Rose refers to as the 'transition generation' of Prime Ministers – Wilson, Heath and Callaghan – who were 'schooled by world depression and war … each raised in a family where pennies had to be counted carefully'. It is this older generation of politicians, according to Rose, who recognised, like the writer himself, that 'policy as well as politics is important'.

Rose goes on to contribute a new phrase to the lexicon of political science: 'intermestic politics'. This, he argues, is the intersection of international and domestic issues and problems that place increased constraints on the modern British Prime Minister. Examples of this include the increasingly complex and, at times fraught nature of membership of the European Union, the development of globalisation and, especially in the case of Tony Blair, the nature of the relationship between America and the rest of the world. The period between July and December 2005 serves as a particularly good example of this as Britain took on the presidency of the European Union at one of the most critical stages in its history, when Blair hosted the G8 summit in Edinburgh to the background noise of Live 8 concerts and associated protests, and as the involvement of British troops in Iraq showed no sign of coming to an end and bombs began to explode on London buses and underground trains. Alongside these issues, Blair faced domestic policy problems with identity cards, a renewal of interest in the number of refugees in Britain and attempts to deliver a workable set of policies to combat antisocial behaviour. As Rose points out, the increased amount of time Prime Ministers are required to spend on these international and intergovernmental issues makes it all the more difficult to be effectively in command of the Westminster/Whitehall policy-making process.

What you should have learnt from reading this chapter

A careful reading of this chapter will have stimulated debate as to the nature of the power of the Prime Minister. We have explained how the debate has been enlivened by the period in office of Tony Blair even though the larger concerns and discussions may be traced back much further into recent history.

The chapter has outlined the powers and roles of the Prime Minister and has also discussed the sources of authority around which these powers are constructed. To balance the discussion we have also looked at the considerable constraints on the power of the Prime Minister and we have listed these constraints in some detail. To illustrate the nature of prime ministerial power we have also summarised the views of Richard Rose and his concept of 'inermestic politics' as an added tool of analysis. Having examined prime ministerial power in some detail, we can now turn our attention to the bureaucracy and support that is available to the holder of this complex and complicated office.

Glossary of key terms

The terms in this glossary refer specifically to the discussion of prime ministerial power. Their meanings may change subtly when applied to other aspects of political study.

Authority The source of prime ministerial powers.

Constitutional/formal powers Those powers historically performed by the monarch and are known as 'prerogative powers' (see below).

Head of government In the United Kingdom – the Prime Minister.

Head of state The person who represents all the people of the state. In the United Kingdom, sometimes it's the Queen, on other occasions it's Tony Blair. This situation has arisen because of the prerogative powers of the Prime Minister.

Intermestic politics A concept developed by Richard Rose. The intersection of international and domestic issues and problems that place increased constraints on the modern British Prime Minister.

Informal/fluid powers As the phrase suggests, these are much more flexible, powers, and the way in which they are exercised reflects greatly on the style and leadership of the Prime Minister. The powers here are mostly those linked with government, and include the political leadership of a party, speaking on behalf of the government and determining government policy.

Prerogative powers The main source of the formal powers of the Prime Minister and derived from those once held by the monarch. Prerogative powers fall into two categories: those performed on behalf of the monarch as head of state and those performed as head of government.

Prime Minister The head of the British government. Since 1997, this position has been held by Tony Blair.

Primus inter pares The belief that in Cabinet, the Prime Minister is 'first among equals'.

? Likely examination questions

Short questions

Describe the origins of the office of Prime Minister.

Briefly describe the formal/constitutional powers of the Prime Minister.

Briefly describe the informal/fluid powers of the Prime Minister.

Describe the main constraints on prime ministerial power.

Explain the difference between external/internal constraints.

Essay questions

'The powers of the Prime Minister are restricted by significant constraints.' To what extent do you agree?

Discuss the main reasons for the increase of the powers of the Prime Minister in recent years.

How far would you agree with the claim that the Prime Minister is too powerful?

Discuss the importance and meaning of prime ministerial power.

Revision task

Research and produce a 'prime ministerial power balance sheet'. For each of the powers that you are able to list, attempt to make a link with one or more constraints on that power.

Helpful websites

www.number10.gov.uk/

www.direct.gov.uk/

www.cabinetoffice.gov.uk/

www.civilservice.gov.uk

www.parliament.uk

Suggestions for further reading

Bagehot, W. (1867, but see also the 1963 edition with Crossman's introduction) *The English Constitution* (Fontana).

Barberis, P. and Carr, F. (2002) 'Executive Control and Dominance under Tony Blair', *Talking Politics*, vol. 12.3, spring 2000.

Benn, T. (1981) *Arguments for Democracy* (Penguin).

Buckley, S. (2004) 'The Hutton Inquiry', *Talking Politics*, vol. 17.1, September 2004.

Burch, M. and Halliday, I. (1996) *The British Cabinet System* (Prentice Hall).

Foley, M. (2000) *The British Presidency* (Manchester University Press).

Foley, M. (2002) *Major, Blair and a Conflict of Leadership: Collision Course* (Manchester University Press).

Johnson, R. W. (1990) 'The President has Landed', *New Statesman*, 30 November 1990.

Kampfner, J. (2003) *Blair's Wars* (Free Press).

McNaughton, N. (1999) *The Prime Minister and Cabinet Government* (Hodder).

Rentoul, J. (2001) *Tony Blair: Prime Minister* (Time Warner).

Rose, R. (2001) *The Prime Minister in a Shrinking World* (Polity Press).

CHAPTER 6

The Prime Minister: Support and Bureaucracy

Contents

Overview

It has already been established that the modern Prime Minister operates as part of an increasingly complex government machine. The position of the British Prime Minister has evolved in such a way as to allow the holder of the office relatively few administrative and bureaucratic resources; it is up to each individual Prime Minister to arrange his or her resources as best they can. Originally, the debate tended to centre around the desirability or otherwise of a 'Prime Minister's Department'. As this now exists in all but name, critics have begun to question the extent to which recent reforms may have compromised sections of Number 10 that were previously intended to be 'non political'. It is these very precise changes within Number 10 itself that we shall focus on in this chapter. The intention here is to establish a clear framework of the bureaucracy of the Prime Minister in such a way as to inform the debates considered in chapters 8 and 9.

Key issues to be covered in this chapter

- The bureaucracy of the Prime Minister
- The role of Downing Street
- Wider means of prime ministerial support
- Lord Birt: case study
- Trends in prime ministerial support
- Should there be a Prime Minister's Department?

The bureaucracy of the Prime Minister

In the British system of government there is no **Prime Minister's Department**. Unlike some foreign political leaders, who are served by bodies staffed by a mixture of appointments both political and administrative, the British Prime Minister is expected to manage both domestic and international spheres of politics without an effectively resourced, staffed or dedicated office. This section of the chapter will examine the complex web of structures that serve as support system and bureaucracy for the modern Prime Minister. We will begin by looking at the structure of 10 Downing Street and the variety of offices contained in that building commonly referred to as the 'Prime Minister's Office'. Following this we will go on to look closely at the less formal means of support that are available to the Prime Minister, mainly through the use of private and individual advisers. We shall also examine the current thinking on the well-established debate around the issue of a Prime Minister's Department.

Downing Street
Approximately 200 people are employed in the various offices that make up 10 Downing Street. When journalists refer to Downing Street they often speak of the 'Prime Minister's Office'. This is not a specific office in the physical sense of the Oval Office in the White House but is rather a collection of resources and arrangements that have evolved over time to support the Prime Minister. When Blair entered Downing Street for the first time in 1997, the Prime Minister's Office consisted of four clearly defined and well-established offices. They were:

- **The Private Office** – management of official engagements and relations with the other parts of government.
- **The Press Office** – management of the relationship between the Prime Minister, government and media.
- **The Political Office** – managed the relationship between the Prime Minister and his or her party and constituency.
- **The Policy Unit** – created in 1974 to provide medium- to long-term policy advice to the Prime Minister.

Earlier, we made distinctions between the powers of the Prime Minister as 'head of state' and 'head of government'. Similarly, it was once possible to distinguish between the various parts of the Prime Minister's Office in Downing Street as either 'official' or 'political'. One of the criticisms of this definition is that, under recent Prime Ministers – notably Thatcher and Blair – the distinctions between the two types of office have not always been clearly defined. This is particularly the case with Blair, where it is best not to be too precious about any 'official/political' division. If we were to stick rigidly to this 'official/political' view and attempt to illustrate it in the form of a simple diagram we would produce something like this:

Box 6.1 Official and Political Number 10

Official Number 10

- Private Office
- Press Office

Political Number 10

- Political Office
- Policy Unit

This is no longer satisfactory. As we have already said, the distinction between 'political' and 'official' has become less and less clear over recent decades, and the distinction has blurred even further in the years since Tony Blair formed his first administration in 1997.

The revised system of secretariats was revealed in June 2001. The BBC News website reflected the general consensus of opinion on the changes when it reported that:

> In a move set to revive criticism over 'Tony's cronies', three new units headed by key allies of Mr Blair are to be set up in 10 Downing Street, while the prime minister's private office and policy unit will merge . . . Mr Blair's official spokesman acknowledged that the changes would mean a rise in the wage bill and number of advisers for Downing Street, both of which have been contentious issues in recent years, but could give neither an overall figure nor individual salaries.

Blair explained the changes as being an essential part of his determination to deliver better public services. In May 2002, less than twelve months after the changes of June 2001, further changes were taking place in the shape of a significant strengthening of the Cabinet Office from which John Prescott was moved into a separate and expanded Deputy Prime Minister's Department. The Cabinet Office, under Lord (Gus) Macdonald (who was not a member of the Cabinet) was henceforth to report back to Tony Blair. Commentators were quick to recognise that this was a final indication that the Cabinet Office was now a resource for the Prime Minister rather than for the Cabinet as a whole. The changes described here are significant to the extent that they caused the majority of commentators to announce the final emergence of a Prime Minister's Department.

It would appear that the Prime Minister's Office is now clearly divided into three sections or 'secretariats'. These are:

- **Policy and Government**, headed by the Chief of Staff, Jonathan Powell.
- **Communication and Strategy**, headed by David Hill.
- **Government and Political Relations**, headed by Ruth Turner.

As we examine these three secretariats in turn, we shall continue to make references to the old system in order to illustrate better the changes that have taken place.

The Prime Minister's Office: Policy and Government

This first section of the post-2001 Prime Minister's Office consists of:

- A combined Private Office and Policy Unit in the single form of a **Policy Directorate**.
- **Prime Minister's Strategy Group**.
- **Delivery Unit**.
- **Office of Public Service Reform**.
- **Honours and Appointments**.
- There are also roles for senior civil servants with specific policy briefs in **Foreign Policy** and **European Policy**.

The Private Office and its key functions appear to have been swallowed up by the Policy and Government branch of the Prime Minister's Office outlined immediately above. In 2001 the Private Office was combined with the Policy Unit to form a Policy Directorate, more of which later. Officials in the old Private Office were usually permanent civil servants 'borrowed' from other government departments, usually for a period of three years. These officials tended to be mid-career, talented, and regarded as 'high fliers'. What was once the separate Private Office continues to deal with the Prime Minister's official engagements and also manages his or her relationship with government departments and Parliament. The Prime Minister's Principal Private Secretary – civil servant, Ivan Rogers – is the head of the Policy Directorate and one of the people closest to the Prime Minister. The position also makes Rogers the third most senior official in the Civil Service (after the Cabinet Secretary and the Permanent Secretary to the Treasury). Beneath the Principal Private Secretary there is a number of other private secretaries who deal with policy areas such as Parliament, home affairs, economics and several more to deal with foreign and international affairs.

It is appropriate to think of the Policy Directorate (and the Private Office that preceded it) as a huge filter of information between the Prime Minister and every other part of the government system. If the Prime Minister wished to be informed and briefed as to the formulation and subsequent development of policy initiatives, then it was the role of the Private Office to provide this information. As we can see, the workings of the Private Office under Blair have changed considerably. It is clear that Jonathon Powell has a major function as Chief of Staff and is essentially the principal 'gatekeeper' of Downing Street and therefore highly influential in deciding who has access to the Prime Minister. His value to Blair is such that it required intervention from the then head of the Civil Service, Sir Robin Butler, to thwart Blair's attempt to have Powell installed as the Principal Private Secretary.

If we turn our attention to trying to understand how and why the directorate functions, it is first necessary to explain the origins and workings of the Policy Unit. It is worth reminding yourself at this point of the very loose nature of the 'official'/'political' distinctions we are making, and the obvious blurring and merging of some roles and responsibilities.

The Policy Unit was created in 1974 by Harold Wilson and has been used in some form by every Prime Minister since. The Policy Unit is designed to provide a more personal resource for the Prime Minister. Wilson felt that, because as there was no separate Prime

Minister's Department, it was necessary for the Prime Minister to have some means of acquiring a strategic view of where the government was heading. With this type of unit the Prime Minister would be able to seek advice on particular aspects of government policy that would help to frame medium-and long-term strategies but would also be on hand for more immediate advice during times of crisis or policy failures. The Policy Unit usually consists of specialists from outside government who are appointed as temporary civil servants normally for the duration of a government, as a new Policy Unit is convened by each incoming Prime Minister. Needless to say, the head of the Policy Unit quickly becomes one of the Prime Minister's key advisers. As we have already mentioned above, the Policy Unit and the Private Office were combined in 2001 to create a Policy Directorate to which we can now turn to examine in more detail.

The Policy Directorate is evidence of Tony Blair's frustration with the way in which the central executive machinery functioned during his first term of office between 1997 and 2001. As we shall see, when combined in the shape of the Policy Directorate, the Policy Unit and the Private Office add another dimension to the debate on the relationship between civil servants and special advisers and the often blurred distinctions between the two.

There is a number of reasons why Prime Ministers need something like that which Blair has in his Policy Directorate and that which his predecessors had in the Policy Unit.

First, this type of office may give the Prime Minister a slight edge in his or her dealings with ministers in providing an alternative source of, and view on, policy issues. As research by Milne has shown, as between 1997 and 2001 the Policy Unit under Blair developed a much deeper role, to the extent that ministers will have been aware that a member of the unit was 'shadowing' each particular policy area.[1] This was not entirely a Blair innovation. The Conservative MP Damien Green carried out a similar function in the Policy Unit of John Major, earning himself the nickname 'spy in the cab' in the process. The role of the Policy Unit in this sense should be clear: it was created to make sure that ministers are working in line with the wishes of Downing Street.

The second reason for the existence and development of this type of office is that it gives the Prime Minister a much more 'immediate' contact with the policy process. Members of the unit/directorate will be consulted on a regular basis by the Prime Minister and will, in some cases, have greater contact with Downing Street than some cabinet ministers have.

Third, the type of office we are discussing is in a powerful position to put forward its own policy initiatives and, in the past, has even championed ideas and policies from outside the political system. Under Thatcher, the Policy Unit was closely linked to the whole philosophical direction of the government through its support for neo-liberal policies in the economy. In fact, the period from 1979 through to the late 1990s saw the Policy Unit steered by a succession of neo-liberal monetarist right wingers – Sir John Hoskyns, Ferdinand Mount, John Redwood and Professor Brian Griffiths – who all contributed to the political complexion of **'Thatcherism'**. Had the Policy Unit not existed, then the connections to the Prime Minister may not have been made, especially by academic outsiders such as Griffiths and the monetarist economic adviser, Sir Alan Walters.

The Policy Unit has also acted as a 'filter' for political ideas and philosophies from other political systems. Writing in 1992, in his book *British Cabinet Government*,[2] James used the moves towards an internal market in the National Health Service as an example of an idea filtered into the policy-making process from the Policy Unit which, in turn, had developed the idea from studies and research in the United States. Blair was no less closely linked to the Policy Unit after 1997 than his predecessors. The unit was first headed by a close associate of the Prime Minister, David Milliband, and, under Blair's direction, took on an even more central role, signified by its physical place in the new machinery of government centred in the Cabinet Office. The creation in 2001 of the Policy Directorate is yet further evidence of a body that had become the personal instrument of prime ministerial domination.

The Prime Minister's Strategy Unit was set up in 2002 to bring together the Performance and Innovation Unit, the Forward Strategy Unit and parts of the Centre for Management and Policy Studies. The Performance and Innovation and Forward Strategy Units were created in 2001 and initially headed by a civil servant, Geoff Mulgan. The Prime Minister's Strategy Unit – according to its web pages – exists to 'provide the Prime Minister and governmental departments with the capacity for longer-term thinking, cross-cutting studies and strategic policy'. Basically, this management unit of the Cabinet Office is tasked with doing the forward thinking of government. Its loose brief is to range widely around a broad swath of policy areas in order to begin the process that may eventually result in legislation and reform up to ten years from now and to function as a 'Centre of Excellence' to 'enhance strategy across government'.

The working parties that are organised by the unit consist of civil servants as well as advisers/academics from outside politics, and produces private reports and strategic audits passed through the Cabinet Secretary for Blair to consider. Recent areas with which the unit has been involved include a digital strategy for the United Kingdom (particularly the exclusion of some groups from the benefits of internet access), a 'strategic audit' of the 'challenges and opportunities facing the UK today' and the proposal of an international strategy to address fragile and unstable countries.

The Delivery Unit is another innovation dating back to the immediate aftermath of the 2001 general election, and was set up under the direction of the Prime Minister's Chief Adviser on Delivery, Professor Michael Barber (who still heads the unit), who was formerly a special adviser to David Blunkett at Education. The role of the unit is straightforward: it exists to ensure that progress is being made on meeting government targets in the improvement of key public services. Working closely with Downing Street, the Treasury, the Cabinet Office and other 'stakeholder' departments, the unit assesses the delivery of, and provides performance management for, key delivery areas. The unit consists of around forty people who represent a broad range of public- and private-sector concerns. Beyond its central core, the unit calls on the expertise of a wider group of 'associates' who have experience in the successful delivery of public, private and voluntary services.

The success of the Delivery Unit is yet to be fully assessed. Reports leaked to the *Guardian* in 2003 suggested that the unit was becoming concerned that the government would not meet its targets on NHS reforms although, by 2004, the unit was more upbeat on this particular issue and briefed journalists that hospitals were now well placed to meet targets on reduced waiting times for operations. Targets to improve the provision of services in transport have been less successful, yet increased internal confidence has led the unit to claim that it is now possible to assess whether individual ministers are doing their job well or not. The unit is starting to dilineate ever more sophisticated details of how departments will be judged on whether they have met targets set out in summer spending reviews, whilst, under Barber, the unit has grown easily into the more traditional aspects of the Civil Service and has avoided upsetting the traditionalists. By late 2004, the unit was broadening its approach to include the problem of increasing numbers of drug users and the problems of child poverty. Irrespective of whatever success the Delivery Unit was able to measure throughout the various Whitehall departments, Barber was left lamenting the scepticism of the public in their perception of Labour's 'revolution' in the delivery of public services. Barber left the Delivery Unit in September 2005 to join the global consultancy, McKinsey's, where he is in charge of providing 'global' advice on public service reform.

The Office of Public Service Reform also dates beck to the 2001 general election. Under the leadership of an ex-Audit Commission civil servant, Wendy Thomson, the office was given the task of pressing ahead with Civil Service reform. The central aim of these reforms was to ensure that government departments would be better equipped to deliver reforms in public services. Like the Delivery Unit and the Prime Minister's Strategy Group, the Office of Public Services Reform is based in the Cabinet Office as part of the Cabinet Secretary's Delivery and Reform Team, yet the head of each has an office within Number 10.

It is important to note at this point that the Office of Public Service Reform and the Delivery Unit are part of the Cabinet Office. This confuses their appearance in the Prime Minister's Office even though the head of each has an office in Downing Street itself. We shall return to the current significance of the Cabinet Office in terms of recent reforms later in this section.

Finally, the Honours and Appointments Secretary deals with all the appointments (mostly non-political) that the Prime Minister is required to make. These appointments will include senior positions in the Church of England along with some university posts and quangos. This particular office is headed by a civil servant. Having looked at the Policy and Government Section of the Prime Minister's Office we may now turn our attention to the second section, Communication and Strategy.

The Prime Minister's Office: Communication and Strategy

Created in 2001, the Communication and Strategy section of the Prime Minister's Office brings together the

- **Press Office**
- **Strategic Communications Unit** and the
- **Research and Information Unit**

Similarly to the way in which we analysed the earlier section on Policy and Government we shall make reference to the origins and history of the three offices that make up the Communication and Strategy section of the Prime Minister's Office to illustrate best how the overall collection of roles and functions have evolved.

Traditionally, the Press Office has been the place where the Prime Minister's relationship with the media is carefully controlled. There have been occasions in the recent past when observers have queried how influential the head of the Press Office – the Press Secretary – has been in terms of the formulation of policy. The post is actually part of the Civil Service yet some Prime Ministers have drawn their Press Secretaries from the media – Joe Haines under Harold Wilson and Alastair Campbell under Blair being two particularly good examples. This is not to say that, when the post has been filled from the Civil Service, it is necessarily less controversial. Bernard Ingham (1979–90) held the post during the Thatcher years. A civil servant, Ingham did much to strengthen the position of the Press Office and was particularly formidable in his handling of journalists and lobby correspondents. While Ingham's influence on policy was minimal (if it existed at all), his forthright and, at times, forceful presentation of government policy frequently gave the impression of someone who had clearly crossed the line of Civil Service neutrality. While not a civil servant, Alastair Campbell was equally criticised during his tenure at the Press Office. With huge influence on the presentation and 'spin' of policy, Campbell had almost unparalleled access to Blair and controlled almost all requests from the media for ministerial interviews. Following the Hutton Inquiry and the subsequent report into the death of the government weapons inspector, David Kelly, Campbell was moved from his position of Press Secretary to a newly created post of Director of Communications and Strategy.

After the 1997 general election, Blair established a Strategic Communications Unit. This was designed to co-ordinate government communications across departments and was attached to the Press Office in Downing Street.

You will recall that, when we were discussing the Office of Public Service Reform and the Policy Directorate in terms of their appearance in both the Cabinet Office and the Prime Minister's Office, we made the point that this confuses the distinction between the Cabinet Office and Number 10. A similar situation emerges when we examine the Strategic Communications Unit. Although the unit is relatively small (around seven members) the make-up is significant in that it includes a mixture of civil servants and political appointees. According to Andrew Turner, this signalled 'Blair's desire for central co-ordination of the government departments' media relations – an aspect of what was referred to as "joined-up government"'. The Strategic Communications Unit was expanded after the 2001 election and was restructured again in early 2004 in line with the recommendations accepted from the Phillis Commission.

By the late spring of 2005 the position now appeared to be split between two individuals with David Hill as the Prime Minister's Director of Communications and Matthew Taylor as Chief Adviser on Strategy.

The Research and Information Unit provides factual information and briefing material to the whole of Number 10.

The Prime Minister's Office: Government and Political Relations

This third section of the Prime Minister's Office consists of:

* **Political Office**
* **Events and Visits Office**
* **Corporate and Direct Communication Units**

Box 6.2 The Prime Minister's Office (June 2005)

Jonathan Powell – Chief of Staff with direct responsibility for leading and co-ordinating operations across Number 10. Powell reports directly to the Prime Minister.
Liz Lloyd – Deputy Chief of Staff.
Ivan Rogers – Principal Private Secretary.
David Hill – Prime Minister's Director of Communications.
Jo Gibbons – Director of Events, Visits and Scheduling.
John McTernan – Director of Political Operations. Provides political management and support for the government's political strategy. (Salary paid by Labour Party.)
David Bennet – Head of Policy Directorate.
Matthew Taylor – Chief Adviser on Strategy.
Ruth Turner – Director of Government Relations.

The Director of Government Relations is the person responsible for the third branch of the Prime Minister's Office – Government and Political Relations – and was established in 2001. The post reflects the importance of the devolved administrations in Scotland, Wales and Northern Ireland. The holder of this post (Ruth Turner in June 2005) has the job of liaising between central government and the various devolved arrangements.

The role of the Political Office (you may still see it referred to as 'Unit') – is to provide liaison and communication between the Prime Minister and the organisation of the political party of which he or she is leader. The office will be in close contact with the headquarters of the political party in power as well as with MPs and party supporters in the constituencies. The office is headed by a Political Secretary, one of the more controversial being Marcia Williams, who worked in the office from 1964 to 1970 and again from 1974 to 1976. Her control of the office and her access to, and influence over, the Labour Prime Minister Harold Wilson are legendary. Though the impact of the office on policy is now felt to be minimal, it is still worth noting how it has been used by some leading political figures as a route into high-level politics. Nigel Lawson and Douglas Hurd worked in the office at different times before going on to rise to Cabinet positions in Conservative governments. Linked to the office is the Prime

Minister's Parliamentary Private Secretary (PPPs) whose job it is to keep the Prime Minister in touch with what is going on along the back benches at Westminster. The office now appears to have evolved into the post of Director of Political Operations and provides, in the words of the Prime Minister's website (www.pm.gov.uk), 'political management and support for the development of the Government's political strategy. The Labour Party pays the salary of the Director.'

The Cabinet Office

We have already outlined the origins and functions of the Cabinet Office in Chapter 3. A more detailed discussion of the Cabinet Office and the Blair reforms will take place in later Chapters.

Wider dimension of support for the Prime Minister

Support mechanisms and sources of advice to the Prime Minister are not exclusively based in and around the established offices and secretariats within Downing Street. Having discussed inner and kitchen cabinets earlier, and having just looked at the 'official'/'political' offices of Downing Street, we can now turn our attention to the wider support networks that a Prime Minister is able to access. Some of these sources, such as personal and individual advisers, will be familiar while others, such as policy agencies and 'think tanks', may be less so.

Personal and individual advisers have been the cause of various kinds of controversy in the recent past. The choice and use of individual advisers are not new. Lloyd George made great use of them during his times as Prime Minister. In many ways, the use of political advisers is as old as politics itself, it is only recently, in an age of greater public knowledge of the individual players in government and power, that the role of advisers has become an issue, particularly where the advice appears to be sought and acted upon over and above the Cabinet (Thatcher), and where the advisers and advice appear to be overconcerned with the manipulation and 'spin' of the political message (Blair).

Tony Blair entered 10 Downing Street with a larger than usual personal staff of more than twenty people, most of them from his opposition private office. As we have already said, political appointees are nothing new yet the scale and number of advisers attending Blair and senior ministers were unprecedented. By 2002 Blair had appointed around twenty-nine advisers, mainly in the Policy Directorate and the Strategic Communications Unit. Critics point to the cost of these advisers (£4.4 million in 2002) alongside a total salary bill for the Prime Minister's Office of about £10.8 million in 1999. The 'revolving-door' nature of some of these appointments has also been questioned. Former advisers have used their positions at Downing Street as a springboard to lucrative careers in the city, most notably Tim Allan (BskyB) and Anji Hunter, Blair's former 'gate-keeper' and personal secretary, who moved to BP as Director of Communications. The most sustained criticism of advisers has been reserved for those closely involved in media relations – the so-called 'spin doctors'.

It is not uncommon to find the work of 'spin doctors' discussed in terms of 'black arts' (Bill Jones), and their influence described as 'obscuring the language of politics' (Joy Johnson, former head of communications for the Labour Party – quoted in Foley). Put simply, the role of spin doctors, who are usually employed by the political parties themselves, is to take the basic message of the government and to make sure it is first 'suitable' for public consumption and to then ensure that the public do, indeed, consume it. For Blair, and this particular type of 'special' adviser, the two individuals who most readily spring to mind are Peter Mandelson and Alastair Campbell.

Mandelson was the central figure in the repackaging and subsequent electoral triumph of 'New' Labour, while Campbell is better known for his work as Press Secretary and later Director of Communications for Blair once the Labour Party was in power. Unelected, with a not altogether distinguished background in tabloid journalism and a brief spell as a writer of soft pornography, Campbell quickly became one of the most powerful people in British politics. With constant access to Blair and virtually complete control over the government's relationship with the media, for a period between 1997 and 2002 many were referring to Campbell as 'the real Deputy Prime Minister'. The issue of individuals such as Campbell achieving high-placed, yet unelected, positions close to the Cabinet was highlighted by the role that Campbell appeared to play in the chain of events that resulted in the suicide of Dr David Kelly, a senior government arms inspector who had worked extensively in Iraq. The subsequent Hutton Inquiry, and Campbell's appearance as a witness before a Commons select committee, did much to throw the focus on Campbell as a key player in the Blair government. Even though exonerated by the subsequent Hutton Report, Campbell had already become concerned over his increasingly visible public role following a television documentary of which he was the subject. By the time of the Hutton Inquiry he had already stepped down from his daily briefings to the press and had taken on the more discreet post of Director of Communications and Strategy.

Rather like Campbell, Peter Mandelson illustrated the value and dangers of the 'private adviser'. Though a Labour MP and therefore, unlike Campbell, elected, Mandelson proved to be a major embarrassment for Blair, resigning not once but twice – on the first occasion because of his failure to disclose a loan from a fellow minister (who was at the time being investigated by the Department of Trade and Industry, the minister for which was Peter Mandelson), and secondly because of his alleged involvement with a plan to assist an Indian billionaire to gain a British passport. The billionaire was also a major donor of cash to the Millennium Dome fiasco. Mandelson's value to Blair should not be underestimated, however. Not only was he a key player in the reinvention of the Labour Party after the election debacles of the 1980s, he was also instrumental in successfully managing Tony Blair's campaign for the party leadership in 1994. Mandelson may have made two grave errors of judgement and may well be beyond any future return to high office in the United Kingdom. He has recently been appointed as the European Union Commissioner for Trade, however, and it may only have been his acceptance of this post that kept him from re-entering the Cabinet for a third time as part of the messy and unwanted reshuffle that was caused by David Blunkett's resignation just before Christmas 2004.

Although the nature of the embarrassments was different from those experienced by Blair over Mandelson and Campbell, Margaret Thatcher experienced her own difficulties with individual advisers. In the 1980s, Sir Alan Walters, a right-wing monetarist economist, already mentioned earlier in relation to the work of policy units, regularly briefed Margaret Thatcher. By 1989, Walters had become such an influence on the development of Margaret Thatcher's economic views that the relationship caused the Chancellor of the Exchequer at that time, Nigel Lawson, to resign. Walters, claimed Lawson, was virtually running the economic policy of the United Kingdom. The issue here of individual advisers is one that brings us back to our earlier discussions of collective cabinet and individual ministerial responsibility. In this case, Lawson clearly felt that his position was being undermined by Walters and that the processes of cabinet discussion and collective responsibility were being bypassed.

While individual and private advisers may occasionally be a controversial part of government, they are nevertheless indispensable to the workings of the higher levels of the executive, and are therefore unlikely to disappear any day soon. The main issue for critics of the existence of these individuals, especially under Blair, is the growing number of them in government (possibly more than eighty in 2000) and the increasingly significant positions they hold as unelected players at the highest level of government. In the case of the New Labour spin doctors, as many have pointed out, these people are essentially civil servants. They may be temporary civil servants, yet, none the less, they are free from the rules that regulate permanent officials and therefore face no requirement to be in any way politically neutral. In the case of one or two of these advisers – certainly Powell and Campbell – Blair has, in the words of Richard Rose: 'leveraged the influence of political appointees through an Order in Council giving two of his senior political advisers (Powell and Campbell) the status of temporary civil servants with authority over career civil servants and also authorising them to act "in a political context" '.[3]

Rose goes on to argue that this expansion of personal advisers and political staff in Downing Street has created friction, not just between officials and advisers, but between players at the highest level of government. We can summarise the involvement of one particular adviser, Lord Birt, in a way that illustrates the arguments framed by Rose.

Case study: Lord Birt and blue sky thinking

By early 2005 the British press seemed to be in agreement that John Birt, the former Director-General of the BBC, had assumed a position as the most influential of all the advisers circling around

Downing Street and Tony Blair. In a private memorandum leaked late in 2004, the then Cabinet Secretary, Sir Andrew Turnbull – the most senior civil servant in the United Kingdom – told senior civil servants in every government department to be more 'strategic' in the way they think about policy. These same civil servants were also told that Lord Birt should be included in discussions about all major proposals for the future.

The memorandum supported the claims being made about the influence of Birt in Downing Street. Birt appears to have replaced Campbell and Mandelson as the Prime Minister's closest confidant on the by now infamous 'sofa'. Originally hired in 2000 to work one day a week, Birt was now a virtually full-time government adviser. The ex-BBC boss has been given an office in Number 10 alongside his former personal assistant, Katie Ray, who is now Blair's diary secretary.

Birt's political presence is significant. He sits in on most of the key political strategy meetings held in Number 10, and sits on the Cabinet Office Strategy and Civil Service Reform programme boards. He will frequently be part of meetings between cabinet ministers and the Prime Minister in discussions about the progress and delivery of government policy, and has produced unpublished reports on antisocial behaviour and on the future development of London. His management style, based on radical, mainly American-originated, management-theory thinking and consultancy-type language (referred to as 'Birtspeak' at the BBC), appeals to a Prime Minister who sees him as someone with the necessary experience of tackling public-service bureaucracy and who wishes to use similar theories and practices to reshape the formulation and development of public services at the highest levels of government. Birt represents two clear issues with the use of personal advisers in the later stages of Blair's premiership.

First, Birt's position emphasises the concerns that people within and without government have expressed for a number of years on the issue of personal advisers. In early 2002, the *Guardian* newspaper used Birt's refusal to give evidence about his ideas on the future of the railways to Gwyneth Dunwoody's Commons Transport Select Committee. In the words of the *Guardian*, the refusal 'may seem a rather petulant dispute between two of the more charm challenged figures in British politics . . . but his [Lord Birt's] refusal, abetted by

Downing Street, is also an important defiance of Parliament'. For critics of the role of personal advisers, the issue illuminates an increasingly important confrontation in relations between the legislature and the executive.

As an adviser to Blair, Birt is not a civil servant, but he is a member of the legislature by virtue of his seat in the House of Lords and is clearly involved in policy making at the highest level. This is, therefore, a similar (if not exactly the same) issue to that illustrated by earlier concerns over the role of Alastair Campbell, and it is a concern based on the lack of accountability. In the system of government that has evolved under Blair, Downing Street advisers now play such as important part in the policy-making process that certain policies carry the imprint of their advice and ideas to the extent that the policies are very different from the originals formulated by government ministers. To use one example, the issue of faith-based schools is an aspect of education policy widely believed to owe far more to the intervention of advisers in Downing Street than to those ideas emerging directly from the Department of Education.

The second issue raised in late-period Blair by the position of Birt is the extent to which his presence illuminates the Tony Blair/Gordon Brown fault-line that lies at the centre of government. In March 2005 it was widely reported that Blair was in the process of considering plans that would involve imposing tighter controls on the Treasury and the senior Civil Service, in an attempt to drive through radical reforms in a third Labour term. Blair had asked Birt to consider plans for the abolition of the Cabinet Office, which has traditionally been the power base of the Civil Service, and for its functions to become part of the revamped Office of the Deputy Prime Minister. It was also reported that, as part of his brief, Birt was looking at the idea of removing key responsibilities from the Treasury as part of a renewed effort to break the political and administrative resistance to the kind of radical reforms that Blair feels have been diluted and delayed in his first two terms.

If the reforms were to go ahead in the way we have outlined, then it is likely that the Prime Minister would emerge with a much clearer control over domestic policy, something that he has had to share with the Chancellor, Gordon Brown, during the first two terms. The plans are essentially an attempt by Blair to challenge Brown's political stronghold in the Treasury in a way that would reduce Brown's strong influence over domestic issues, particularly welfare, civic renewal, the labour market, energy and transport – all areas that Birt has 'advised' on in recent years.

If successfully introduced, the proposals that Birt has been considering (according to some Number 10 insiders, the ideas were being discussed as far back as 2000–1) would substantially concentrate power inside Number 10 and would settle the issue of a Prime Minister's Department (see below) once and for all.

Birt's involvement with this particular aspect of 'blue sky thinking' has thrown into focus all the debates and concerns that surround the use of special advisers. The Liberal Democrat MP, Norman Baker, wrote to the Cabinet Secretary pointing out that, in addition to his unpaid work at Number 10, Lord Birt is a paid adviser to the management consultants, McKinsey. Baker called for Birt to be investigated for potential conflict of interest, and referred to Birt's role in government as being 'entirely improper'.

Trends in prime ministerial support

We now need to make some summary points about the nature of the bureaucracy and support that surround the Prime Minister. Research by Kavanagh and Seldon[4] has examined the growth of the bureaucracy in Downing Street over recent years. We shall return to some of their findings later in the book when we discuss the 'presidential' debate surrounding the Prime Minister but, in the light of what we have already said on this matter, it will be useful now to highlight the trends that Kavanagh and Seldon have recorded:

- The number of people in Number 10 has grown significantly – seventy-one in 1970, 150 in 1999 – this has produced an 'institutionalism' and 'collectivism' of the premiership: an ever-increasing number of people are speaking and writing in his/her name.
- The 'official' and 'political' offices of Number 10 are starting to overlap (we have already shown how this has continued apace in the time since this research was published). This overlap presents opportunities for the kind of 'turf disputes' noted above and, in the

vivid description of Clare Short, the 'entourages at war for their prince'.

- Officials have gradually become more comfortable with political appointees. The pre-Blair convention of appointing special or political advisers only to the Policy Unit and Political Office is now largely forgotten. There is something approaching large-scale recruitment of political elements in Number 10 with Blair's appointments of staff and advisers similar to that of a new US President introducing a new team to the White House.

- The Prime Minister is increasingly drawn to what Kavanagh and Seldon refer to as his Number 10 office where his staff work on his behalf. This pulls the Prime Minister away from Cabinet and Parliament.

Should there be a Prime Minister's Department?

The smart answer to this may well be: 'there already is one'. In this section we shall examine the debate surrounding the issues of a Prime Minister's Department before discussing the arguments for and against. We shall then make the case that, essentially, Tony Blair has finished the process started by his predecessors and has, in fact, created a *de facto* Prime Minister's Department.

The argument was once put forward that the Prime Minister operated at a certain disadvantage when compared to his key colleagues in the Cabinet and when compared to heads of government elsewhere. The Chancellor in Germany has a large executive staff and office as does the Taoiseach in Ireland. The President of the United States has considerable executive support, as does the French President. The British Prime Minister, however, is faced with making whatever he or she may from the collection of offices in 10 Downing Street and the presence of the Cabinet Office. Those who have argued for the creation of a Prime Minister's Department have done so on the basis that such a development would be of great benefit to central government because it would give Prime Ministers the support they needed to speak on behalf of the government on a wide range of issues. Sir Keith Berrill, a former head of the Central Policy Review Staff has put forward a similar argument. As we shall go on to argue, however, in the words of a source close to Tony Blair quoted by Peter Hennessey: 'it [the debate over a Prime Minister's Department] is largely academic – we already have one'.[5] We can turn first to the arguments for and against this particular development.

Arguments for:

- The Prime Minister needs more resources to help manage the growing demands on his or her time. These demands will continue to grow, so the system should formalise a clear support network through a Prime Minister's Department.
- A Prime Minister's Department would allow the holder of the office to more effectively to represent the government to the world.
- The increased policy workload of modern government requires a Prime Minister to be able to give strategic direction and cohesion to the policy process.
- Cabinet ministers have large-scale administrative support from their officials, and many appoint their own special advisers. Cabinet committees may also act occasionally as alternative power bases to Number 10. On the other hand, support for the Prime Minister may be considered less permanent and more difficult to control.
- The basis of a Prime Minister's Department already exists, so why not simply formalise (and therefore make accountable) what has happened by default.

Arguments against:

- The Prime Minister may 'lose touch' with the rest of government.
- A Prime Minister's Department may well result in the weakening of the powers of the Prime Minister because the flexible arrangements of the current system would be lost to the more rigid structures of a formal and hierarchical bureaucracy.
- How would a Prime Minister's Department fit into the hierarchy of Cabinet? What relationship, for instance, would a junior minister in the Prime Minister's Department have with permanent secretaries in other departments and with other cabinet ministers?
- The Prime Minister may use his or her department as an opportunity to develop a political agenda that might be different from that of other cabinet ministers. Because it would be a bureaucratic structure, it would develop a culture and mentality of its own that might result in the Prime Minister being offered only one argument

or one course of action. There would also be the danger here that one person might come to dominate the Prime Minister in terms of access and information, as opposed to the loose groups around Number 10 at the moment.

- The department would simply produce more paperwork that the Prime Minister would find it almost impossible to deal with.

- A Prime Minister's Department would be a major revolution in the structure of the Constitution and could easily be interpreted as a formal declaration of a move from a cabinet system, based on individual and collective responsibility, to one based on prime ministerial government.

In fact, as we have already said, it is possible to argue that a Prime Minister's Department does exist in all but name. We can now list the key pieces of evidence to support this argument.

Perhaps the strongest single piece of evidence can be drawn from the reforms put into place by Blair in the spring and early summer of 2002, and referred to in various parts of this book. We have already established that the centralising tendency of Blair had been pointing in this direction since his entry to government in 1997, yet it was to be the events of early 2002 that finally revealed the extent of his reforming ambition. As we have seen, in the immediate aftermath of the 2001 election, Blair established the three secretariats, which themselves built on earlier reforms, such as the Strategic Communications Unit, the expanded Cabinet Office and the proliferation of units and task forces to help create what some observers were referring to by 2001 as the 'mosaic' at the centre of British government.

In May 2002, the Transport Minister, Stephen Byers, resigned from the Cabinet following a range of problems in his department, not least the sustained failure to 'deliver' in key areas of transport policy. The reshuffle that followed the resignation of Byers gave Blair the opportunity to dismantle the huge department of transport, local government and the regions, handing what the BBC political web-correspondent described as the 'poison chalice' of transport to the 'capable Brownite, Alistair Darling'. It was to be the reforms to the Cabinet Office, however, especially the promotion of the Blair loyalist Lord Macdonald, that would, in effect, create a Prime Minister's Department in Whitehall that would allow Macdonald to 'spread his tentacles' [Nick Assinder] into every Whitehall department and report directly to Blair.

As the dust settled on the hasty reshuffle, it was left to John Prescott, the Deputy Prime Minister, to encapsulate the significance of what had happened. Prescott defended Byers against those Labour MPs whom he accused of 'plunging the knife' into the Transport Secretary during select committee criticisms of the government's ten-year transport plan while admitting at the same time that the government had, indeed, failed to deliver in key areas. Prescott had emerged as one of the 'winners' in the reshuffle. By arranging that the Cabinet Office could now focus almost entirely on the monitoring of the delivery of public services, Blair had handed Prescott the department functions of the Cabinet Office. Speaking in a radio interview, Prescott praised Blair's decision to focus the work of the Cabinet Office on delivery and welcomed the establishment of a 'Prime Minister's Department' before going on to say that: 'the Prime Minister is a man who likes to be hands-on . . . therefore you have a department geared to meet those needs'.

Even with this unequivocal endorsement from the Deputy Prime Minister, Downing Street was still sensitive to the implications of Prescott's comments, especially as it had always insisted it would not breach constitutional convention by setting up a Prime Minister's Department.

The reforms did not meet with the approval of everyone. The Commons Public Administration Committee had already urged Blair to break with precedent and face questions about the power of Number 10 staff. Tony Wright, the chairman of the committee, said:

> What this confirms is that there is a Prime Minister's Department in all but name, with a growing capacity to drive policy from the centre. We [the Public Administration Committee] will be renewing our invitation to the Prime Minister to attend the select committee to account for the structure and operation of the new Downing Street.

Wright renewed his attack in the aftermath of the 2002 reforms and called for a bill that would sort out the problems between civil servants and special advisers.

Some observers were slightly less measured in their assessment of the 2002 changes. Sir Richard Packer, the permanent secretary at the

Ministry of Agriculture between 1993 and 2000 claimed that Downing Street was operated along the lines of Nazi Germany. According to Packer, Blair's government: '. . . reminded me of the Third Reich where there were overlapping responsibilities and nobody would know where ultimate responsibility lay'.

Speaking to the BBC's *On The Record*, Packer went on to express concern about the way power had been seized from departments, and the way in which power was increasingly concentrated at the centre. Lord Butler, head of the Civil Service between 1988 and 1998, also contributed to the debate by warning that the impartiality of the Civil Service was at risk by the appointment of special advisers with political affiliations. There have been other views on the reforms:

- Holliday argued that the increased integration and co-ordination of the Prime Minister's Office and the Cabinet Office under Blair has made them 'a single executive office'.[6]
- Blair has significantly strengthened the resources available to the Prime Minister between 1997 and 1999, again in 2001, and once more in 2002. The 2002 reforms are particularly significant. As we have already pointed out, his main aim is to achieve the greater link between policy and presentation and to achieve the kind of integration between private office and policy unit in such a way that delivery will be improved.
- The creation of units on social exclusion and policy innovation has been designed in such a way as to keep the Prime Minister fully in the policy loop, and to give clear lines of responsibility and reporting right back to Downing Street.

••

✅ What you should have learnt from reading this chapter

- Although the picture is yet to be thrown fully into focus (and the aftermath of the 2005 election victory may yet yield further changes), it is clear beyond doubt that the resources available to the Prime Minister have undergone a fundamental shift.

- The role of the Cabinet Office has undergone major reform. It exists now in such a way as to serve the Prime Minister rather than the Cabinet as a whole.

- The British Prime Minister is now supported by something similar to the Executive Office of the President in the United States.

- Under Blair, the various offices in Number 10 and the reformed Cabinet Office represent something very similar to the official Prime Minister's Departments in New Zealand and Australia.

- Further reform may yet be in the pipeline. In March 2005, the *Daily Telegraph* was predicting a possible cabinet position for Lord Birt that would give him the job of shaking up Whitehall departments and the Civil Service to drive through reform. The article 'Blair Plans Exit Strategy to Ensure Reform' (Helm and Sylvester) also predicted the emergence of an official Prime Minister's Department in the shape of a 'beefed-up' Cabinet Office with enhanced strategy and delivery units, giving it greater control over individual departments.

Glossary of key terms

Blue sky thinking The attempt to think beyond the normal constraints of short-term demands in an effort to plan policies for the future.

Prime Minister's Department The much-discussed reform that would give the Prime Minister a department and staff similar to that enjoyed by other cabinet ministers. Under Blair, a Prime Minister's Office has effectively been created, even though it doesn't 'exist' as such.

Spin-doctors Mostly used as a derogatory term to describe political media managers (or media manipulators, as their detractors would claim).

Thatcherism The term coined to describe the neo-liberal, right-wing and monetarist philosophies of Margaret Thatcher: Prime Minister 1979–90.

Likely examination questions

Short questions

Provide brief descriptions of the roles of the following:

>   Policy Directorate
>   Prime Minister's Strategy Group
>   Delivery Unit
>   Office of Public Service Reform
>   Honours and Appointments
>   Press Office
>   Strategic Communications Unit
>   Research and Information Unit
>   Political Office.

Why are specialist and personal advisers criticised?

Briefly describe the informal/fluid powers of the Prime Minister.

Describe the role of Lord Birt and the criticisms that he has attracted.

Briefly summarise the arguments for and against a Prime Minister's Department.

Essay questions

To what extent, and why, has Tony Blair increased the power of Number 10?

How far would you agree with the suggestion that the Prime Minister has more resources at his disposal now than in 1997?

'Tony Blair has delivered joined-up government.' Discuss.

'Special advisers are not a welcome addition to the system of government.' How far do you agree?

Discuss the claim that the office of the Prime Minister is now served by a Prime Minister's Department.

'A Prime Minister's Department is unnecessary and unwanted.' Discuss.

Revision task

Use an A3 sheet of paper to sketch the key components of the three secretariats in the Prime Minister's Office. Label the sketch carefully, then explain the role and function of each part of the structure on a separate sheet of paper. Use a highlighter pen to indicate those parts of the structure that have been introduced by Tony Blair.

 Helpful websites

www.number10.gov.uk/

www.direct.gov.uk/

www.cabinetoffice.gov.uk/

http://news.bbc.co.uk

The BBC website is particularly good for tracking the various changes in central government.

http://politics.guardian.co.uk

An excellent website for political analysis.

Suggestions for further reading

Barberis, P. and Carr, F. (2002) 'Executive Control and Dominance under Tony Blair', *Talking Politics*, vol. 12.3, spring 2000.

Burch and Haliday (1996) *The British Cabinet System* (Harvester).

Burnham, J. and Jones, G. (2000) 'Advising the Prime Minister', *Talking Politics*, vol. 12.2, winter 2000.

Foley, M. (2000) *The British Presidency* (Manchester University Press).

Foley, M. (2002) *Major, Blair and a Conflict of Leadership: Collision Course* (Manchester University Press).

Hennessy, P. (2002) 'The Blair Government in Historical Perspective', *History Today*, January 2002.

Jackson, N. (2003) 'The Blair Style – Presidential, Bilateral or Trilateral Government?', *Talking Politics*, vol. 15.3, January 2003.

James, S. (1992) *British Cabinet Government* (Routledge).

Jones, A. (2002) 'Special Advisers and the Demise of Sir Humphrey?', *Talking Politics*, vol. 15.1, September 2002.

Kampfner, J. (2003) *Blair's Wars* (Free Press).

Kavanagh, D. (2000) 'The Power Behind the Prime Minister', *Talking Politics*, vol. 12.3, spring 2000.

Kavanagh, D. (2001) 'Tony Blair as Prime Minister', *Politics Review*, vol. 11.1, September 2001.

Milne, K. (1998) 'The Policy Unit', *New Statesman*, July 1998.

Rentoul, J. (2001) *Tony Blair: Prime Minister* (Time Warner).

Rose, R. (2001) *The Prime Minister in a Shrinking World* (Polity).

Turner, A. (2003) 'Is there a Prime Minister's Department?', *Politics Review*, vol. 12.3, February 2003.

The Prime Minister and Style

Contents

Overview

In the previous two chapters we examined the structural and institutional bases of prime ministerial power. By analysing the ways in which recent Prime Ministers have used the various official and semi-official support systems available to them, we have constructed an overview of the distribution and application of political power at the very highest level of the British political system. It should be apparent from our discussions so far that the exercise of political power by the Prime Minister has varied from administration to administration. A number of longer-term trends towards centralisation and prime ministerial methods of government may be becoming apparent, yet it is also important to recognise that the management of the executive and the use of political power are also determined to a large extent by the personality, leadership skills and overall 'style' of the head of the government. It is to a more detailed discussion of prime ministerial style that we now turn.

Key issues to be covered in this chapter

- Why the study of prime ministerial style is important
- The distinction between style and personality
- Political style as political skill
- The Blair, Thatcher and Major styles

Why is style important?

The analysis of leadership **style** has grown substantially in recent years as the opportunities to study prime ministerial style have increased. The increased intensity of the twenty-four-hour rolling-news-fuelled media speculation of modern politics coupled with the proliferation of memoirs and published diaries from former ministers and advisers have allowed much more information about the style of individual Prime Ministers into the public domain than was once the case.

As we have mentioned elsewhere, Richard Rose has classified the three most recent Prime Ministers, Thatcher, Major and Blair, as the 'television' generation of political leaders.[1] This distinction between earlier holders of the post is significant when examining prime ministerial styles, yet also adds a note of caution to the whole exercise. When analysing 'style', it becomes important to be lucid about exactly what is being discussed under that heading and to make clear distinctions between 'style' and 'personality' even though the two factors will invariably be linked.

When discussing the 'style' of recent Prime Ministers, we shall be looking mainly at the ways in which they have functioned in the role of Prime Minister. It is the case that each Prime Minister leaves his or her mark on the exercise of power and that each Prime Minister has at times subtle, and at other times widely different, approaches to the management of the executive. Discussions of 'style' will therefore include:

- Conduct of and approaches to policy formulation and policy management.
- Conduct of and approaches to the formal role of head of state, with particular emphasis on the conduct of foreign affairs and relations.
- Conduct of and approaches to policy presentation and management of the media.
- Conduct of and approaches to cabinet management.
- Conduct of and approaches to ideology and party political programmes.

Style as personality

It should be instantly recognisable that it is difficult to analyse a Prime Minister in terms of the various conducts and approaches set out above without bringing the personality of the Prime Minister into the equation. It may be said, for instance, that the political and leadership style of Margaret Thatcher was framed by a very distinctive personality. Likewise, when observed from the point of view of 'style', the premiership of Tony Blair almost invariably invites discussion of his personality. The emphasis on personality in recent years may be explained by a number of factors:

- **The impact of television and the need for the Prime Minister to be a polished and accomplished media performer** The kind of exposure that a modern Prime Minister can expect to receive on television has made analysis of, and comment on, them as 'personalities' regular aspects of political discussion. This is particularly the case during election campaigns when opinion polls choose to focus certain questions on the electorate's perception of individual leaders (see below). This invites judgements on personality and appearance, often at the expense of the issues.

- **The modern cult of celebrity has now enveloped the political** This may not be entirely the modern phenomenon we think it is. Political figures in the nineteenth century, for instance, were no less 'popular' public figures than those whom we have today, yet the modern politician can easily expect to be subjected to far closer scrutiny and forensic-like examination than was ever the case for Gladstone or Disraeli. Politicians themselves do little to reverse this trend. Party managers now seek celebrity endorsements as an essential part of any election campaign, and political leaders are usually eager to appear alongside the same celebrity figures in an attempt to tap into what may be a reflected 'glow' that characterises celebrity figures. In the early days of Blair's first administration, for instance, the brief attempt to repackage Britain as 'Cool Britannia' and weave the government into the general *Zeitgeist* of 'Britpop' was a fairly cynical attempt to exploit a particular moment of cultural 'cool' for the purpose of emphasising the essential 'newness' of 'New' Labour. Inviting Oasis to Downing Street was therefore an attempt to exploit the cachet of modern celebrity and invariably invited the media to become focused on the personalities and private lives of politicians in precisely the same way as they were already doing with pop stars, soap actors and reality TV contestants. In the political sense, the style of a Prime Minister may well be, among other things, about leadership, co-ordination and management, but it is also about his or her personality.

Not all political commentators agree that the study of leadership styles is significant, nor has there been any systematic attempt to examine the nature of prime ministerial styles over a sustained period. Michael Burch has argued that it is difficult to make accurate assessments of prime ministerial style, and that the central problem in attempting to put together a generally accepted means of classifying styles and personalities is the lack of genuine evidence. No senior politician would ever take part in a study by a combination of political analysts and clinical psychologists in an effort to produce an accurate personality profile. This does not stop people trying however. In the run up to the 2005 general election campaign, the opinion polls often asked the type of question that could be answered only by a rapid reflection on the personality of the Prime Minister rather than through any considered and thoughtful analysis of the issues. A sample of the questions that came under the broad heading of Blair's approval rating should illustrate the point:

- Populus: Do you think that the following people have a likeable personality or not? (Tony Blair: Yes, 49 per cent; No, 44 per cent.) December 2004.
- ICM: Which of the following statements do you think could be applied to the Prime Minister, Tony Blair? 'Has lots of personality' (Yes, 54 per cent.) July 2004.
- YouGov: Which of these words and phrases apply to Tony Blair? 'Principled' (Yes, 28 per cent.) October 2004.
- ICM: Which of the following statements do you think could be applied to the Prime Minister, Tony Blair? 'Too Presidential'. (Yes, 62 per cent.) July 2004.
- ICM: Which of the following statements do you think could be applied to the Prime Minister, Tony Blair? 'Arrogant'. (Yes, 50 per cent.) February 2005.
- YouGov: Which of these words and phrases apply to Tony Blair? 'Arrogant'. (Yes, 39 per cent.) October 2004.

- Populus: Do you think Tony Blair has a vision of where he wants to lead the country? (Yes, 65 per cent; No, 32 per cent.) May 2004.
- YouGov: Which of these words and phrases apply to Tony Blair? 'Moderate'. (Yes, 21 per cent.) October 2004.
- ICM: Which of the following statements do you think could be applied to the Prime Minister, Tony Blair? 'Trustworthy'. (Yes, 30 per cent.) February 2005.

Clearly, the respondents to these types of question are, first and foremost, more likely to be making immediate responses based on their perceptions of Blair's personality. It is also important to point out that the real picture of whatever constitutes the genuine 'style' and 'personality' of any given Prime Minister is difficult to assess accurately for two key reasons:

- There is much information to which we simply do not have access.
- The personality and style traits of the Prime Minister are spun and distorted by the party and by the media.

In general terms, the classic study of prime ministerial style remains Norton's fourfold typology:[2]

Norton is not providing a definitive model of prime ministerial styles, more a focus for future inquiry. He points out, for instance, that the four categories are not mutually exclusive and argues that all Prime Ministers exhibit a preponderance of characteristics of a particular type. Thatcher, for instance, provides us with a classic example of the innovator. Her vision of politics was based on a radical approach: that she alone instinctively felt that the country needed to move in a new direction; that a whole new attitude of mind was required; and that she was the person who would act as the catalyst for this change. So, for Norton, the typology he offers us comes with a safety warning – we must bear in mind two key qualifications when we use his model:

- Prime Ministers may appear in more than one of the four parts of the typology.
- Prime Ministers may 'drift' between parts of the typology and adopt a particular style to suit a particular set of circumstances.

Andrew Heywood has offered a slightly different model in which he has identified three main leadership styles that Prime Ministers display.[3]

Box 7.1 Prime ministerial styles (Norton, 1987)

Innovators

For the innovator, power is the means by which some future goal may be achieved.

Most innovators are driven by some degree of ideological motivation.

The innovator may not have the support of all parts of their party. The ideas and policies of the innovator may be formulated outside the party and may not have the agreement of all factions and groups within the party.

Under the innovator, the main body of party and government policy is personified by their personality and style.

Reformers

Like the innovator, the reformer seeks to achieve power in order to deliver a future goal.

Like the innovator, reformers are ideologically motivated.

Unlike the innovator, the reformer will have had his or her policy goals formulated and agreed by the party.

Unlike the innovator, the policies and goals of the reformer will not necessarily reflect their personality and style.

Egoists

For the egoist political power is an end in itself.

The egoist seeks to gain power and to then retain and exercise that power for as long as possible.

Egoists tend to see the exercise of power as an activity that exists in the present and with short-term goals. The egoist is

Balancers

Political stability, peace and continuity are the key goals of the balancer.

The balancer seeks this stability in both his or her party and in society as a whole.

Norton argues that balancers fall into two subcategories:

1   Those who actively seek office in an attempt to bring some stability to what may be a volatile situation.

less interested in long-term planning and future goals. The egoist is motivated more by self-regard and the desire for power in itself – ideology is rarely a major motivating force for the egoist.	2 Those who find themselves in power usually as a result of having played the role of a 'compromise' or 'conscript' candidate in leadership elections.

The *laissez-faire* Prime Minister

The type of Prime Minister who exhibits *laissez-faire* tendencies is essentially a 'hands-off' manager who allows cabinet ministers to get on with their departmental responsibilities with little or no interference. Sir Alec Douglas Home, the Conservative Prime Minister for a brief period in the 1960s, is probably the classic example of this type of approach.

The transactional Prime Minister

This type of Prime Minister sees his or her main role as 'honest broker' between senior colleagues in Cabinet. The main aim of the transactional Prime Minister is to maintain the unity of the government. Harold Wilson, Labour Prime Minister in the 1960s, and 1970s, is usually regarded as the epitome of the transactional leader.

The transformational Prime Minister

If we use the model today, it is possible to make a case for Tony Blair falling into this category. This type of Prime Minister leads the Cabinet in a particular direction through some form of ideological conviction. The other obvious contender for an appearance in this category is Margaret Thatcher. More of Thatcher later in this chapter.

Style and skill

When discussing style we are, in fact, making assessments of political skill. It is likely to be the case that those Prime Ministers who have the less successful political careers may well be judged as having the least successful style, and vice versa. When we go on to provide more detailed analyses of individual Prime Ministers later in this chapter, we shall say more about individual skills. As part of this general overview of style, personality and skill, however, it may be useful to make some general points on political skill.

In the essay we have already referred to in our discussion of the fourfold typology, Norton goes on to identify three key skills which most Prime Ministers will need from time to time.[4]

'Impression management'

This is largely what you might imagine. Prime Ministers need to give the 'right impression'. This means that they must be convincing in their role as Prime Minister. Blair appears still to be able to project this particular quality and skill as did Thatcher for most of her time as Prime Minister. John Major began to lose this skill fairly quickly and it is questionable as to whether James Callaghan ever had it.

'Feel for office'

This skill is all about intuition, about knowing when to use particular skills in certain circumstances and about knowing where, when and how to 'do the right thing' to achieve whatever aims he or she may have.

'Leading and reacting'

This skill is about knowing when to adopt the appropriate role for a given set of circumstances. These roles may include 'the commander', 'the persuader', 'the negotiator', 'the manager' and the 'manipulator'. The successful 'leading and reacting' Prime Minister will also know when to 'hide' at the appropriate time during a policy crisis that he or she does not wish to be associated with.

If it is difficult then effectively to assess the style and personality of a Prime Minister in office, might it be possible to gain insight from his or her behaviour in opposition or earlier in their government careers?

Style in Opposition

Behaviour in opposition does not always indicate how an individual will behave in power. As leader of the Opposition during Major's government, however, Blair appears to have been very aware of the difference between himself and the Prime Minister in terms of their relationships with their parties, even going so far as to comment in Parliament: 'I lead my party, he follows his.' It is worth noting that, historically, the Labour Party has been suspicious of this type of leadership since the 1930s when Ramsay MacDonald employed a similar style to such an extent that the party was very nearly split.

Blair's style as Prime Minister has almost certainly been conditioned by his own experiences in opposition, and by the larger experiences of the Labour Party during the years 1979 to 1997 and the four general election defeats that mark this period. The despair in the Labour Party, especially following the fourth successive election defeat in 1992 and the sudden death of the new leader John Smith in 1994, was such that Blair was able quickly to dominate the party and get his own way on the revival and reorganisation of policy and presentation. In its embryonic phase, Blair's leadership style was therefore as much a product of the contemporary Labour Party as it was a reflection of his personality and character.

Opposition can also influence leadership style in terms of the historical distance it may place between the potential leader and the actual exercise of power. When, for instance, Blair became Prime Minister in 1997, it was on the back of a long period of opposition for his party (already explained above) and, he had had no experience whatsoever of government. This has not been the case for most of Britain's modern Prime Ministers. Major, Thatcher, Callaghan, Heath and Wilson all had had opposition and government experience before entering Downing Street as Prime Minister. When Blair entered Downing Street himself, therefore, he felt no historical or party attachment to the traditional structures of power nor did his observation of Major's government after 1992 give him any sense that the same structures and practices were in any way effective.

There is evidence that the Blair style of leadership and attitude to the exercise of power were well established before 1997. Peter Mandelson, along with Rod Liddle, who was later to be appointed by Blair to the Policy Unit, published *The Blair Revolution* in 1996 and made no secret of the kind of government that Blair would lead nor the type of leadership he would exercise in doing so. On the eve of the 1997 election, Blair could have been no clearer as to his leadership style when he used a speech to make the point that 'people have to know that we will run from the centre and govern from the centre'. Mandelson and Liddle had been saying much the same thing twelve months previously when they wrote: 'He [Blair] has to get control of the central government machine and drive it hard in the knowledge that if the government does not run the machine the machine will run the government.'[5] As other commentators have pointed out: Blair's style of leadership in government closely resembles that of his leadership in opposition, and that has been both a strength and a weakness.

One further factor relating to opposition and style should be mentioned here and it connects to the point made above about Blair's complete lack of government experience. When Blair appointed his first Cabinet in 1997, it was as inexperienced as the Prime Minister himself. A small handful of ministers had had some junior experience in the Callaghan government before 1979, yet the vast majority was not even in Parliament at that time let alone in Cabinet. Blair's ministers, therefore, had never had the opportunity to establish for themselves any kind of ministerial track record or reputation. It is understandable to see the likelihood of Blair deciding that there was no reason to treat his colleagues as cabinet ministers in any way differently from how he had handled them as members of the Shadow Cabinet.

Having given a brief overview of some of the key theories and indicators of prime ministerial style, we may now go on to discuss specific examples from the careers of the three most recent Prime Ministers. We will begin by looking at Tony Blair in much more detail.

The case of Tony Blair as Prime Minister: a 'tousled efficiency'

One of the earlier studies of Blair's personality and style was by Norman Fairclough who described Blair's leadership as 'immensely successful'.[6] In his study and in a detailed analysis of Blair's broadcast at the time of the death of the Princess of Wales, Fairclough made much of Blair's skills and style as a political communicator. Fairclough makes the point that, on this particular occasion, Blair's style mixed words and 'bodily performance' in what was a largely successful attempt to capture the national mood. This aspect of Blair's leadership has been a key factor in analysing his style and has been employed time and time again, most recently in the immediate aftermath of the terrorist attacks on London in July 2005. Fairclough asked the question:

> Why are these words so effective in 'striking a chord' with many people? One important point is that it was not just his words but his overall bodily performance, the way he looked and acted, as well as what he said. But the language was an important factor.

Fairclough goes on to say that:

> A crucial part of the success and apparent continuing popularity of Blair's style is his capacity to, as it were, 'anchor' the public politician in the 'normal person' – the necessary posturing and evasions of politics are it seems at least partially redeemed by Blair's capacity to reassert constantly his normal, decent, likeable personality. In his speeches and interviews there is always a mix between the vernacular language of the normal person and the public language of politics. The sort of 'normal person' that comes across is very much 'middle-class' and 'middle-England' in values, outlook and style.

By 2004, the Blair style of government, as opposed to the more 'personality'-based analysis of Fairclough, was facing substantial criticism. The Butler and Hutton reports both highlighted the 'informal' style of Blair's 'sofa culture' and informal machinery of government in less than glowing terms. Criticism of Blair in terms of his leadership style have been particularly vocal in the period since British involvement in the war in Iraq, and the issue of Blair's integrity and trust became key factors in the 2005 general election.

As we have already pointed out, Blair is the epitome of the new-style, television-age Prime Minister. In the study by Rose already mentioned, the key features of this type of Prime Minister include:

- Less time spent in the House of Commons.
- Less time spent in long cabinet meetings (the modern Prime Minister thinks they're a waste of time).
- Awareness of the power of the modern media and the importance of the political message.
- More time spent with concentric circles of confidants and advisers.
- At ease with the blurred distinction between civil servant and appointed political advisers that they themselves have been largely responsible for.

- A greater role for political staff in the Prime Minister's Office, and the relaxed approach to making these appointments 'temporary' political servants willing to act in a political context.

As we have seen above, early contributions to the debate surrounding Tony Blair's prime ministerial style focused very much on Blair's 'strong' leadership and communication skills built on what was a commanding parliamentary position. We may summarise these views of the political and leadership style of early period Blair as follows:

- **A good communicator** with a very good instinct for defining the national mood. This skill and this style were also evident in what was a very well-defined **charisma** based on an even stronger political foundation than that enjoyed by Margaret Thatcher.

- **A willingness to accept mistakes and to apologise**, as in the case early in the first administration of the money accepted by the Labour Party from Formula One racing and the subsequent government exemption for the sport from a ban on tobacco advertising.

- **The ability to 'hide'**, as we discussed above, was also evident in the early years of Blair's leadership. Even when Blair found it difficult to distance himself from some of the problems and crises that beset his government during the first two years of power, his personal popularity rating suffered very little.

- **The air of certainty**, the almost palpable 'I know we are right' conviction of Blair in the early period of his premiership reminded observers of Thatcher at the peak of her own political powers. This sense of conviction and destiny was in sharp contrast to the uncertainty and lack of direction that characterised Major's later years in power.

- **A clear sense of 'being in charge'** – again, similar to Thatcher but very different from Major, especially in terms of his relationship with the Cabinet. Some commentators, such as Peter Hennessey, did not always interpret this facet of Blair's style as being necessarily a positive factor. In abandoning the collegiate/collective style for one that was primarily 'command and control', he was attempting to develop a populist style whereby the government was largely identified with Blair personally. As we shall see, this particular argument, along with others, will be a key piece of evidence in the case against Blair when we move on to discuss the more substantial debate on his actual methods of governing.

In an article written before the attacks on the World Trade Center in 2001, Kavanagh attempted to place Blair in some historical perspective. He wrote: 'Blair has yet to be tested by crises comparable to those which the outstanding leaders faced, and his long term influence on the agenda can only be judged when he leaves office.'[7] It is probably fair to argue that, since September 2001, Blair has indeed been tested by a series of crises that, in the long run, will come to define his leadership style.

Blair's leadership style, and very possibly his political legacy, have been transformed by the events since September 2001. It is fair to say that Blair was no stranger to war before these events. As John Kampferer has pointed out, Blair had a remarkable record of involvement in foreign wars that included Kosovo and Sierra Leone. His involvement in the 'war on terror', however, has eclipsed all of these. Moreover, the evidence that emerged in the Hutton and Butler inquiries has revealed much more about the political style and workings of the Blair court than was ever revealed before. The post-2001 Blair style may be summarised as follows:

- **The war leader** – the events associated with the attacks on America in 2001 and the subsequent 'war on terrorism' will undoubtedly become Blair's defining themes as Prime Minister. For most of his second administration, Blair focused on foreign policy issues and the war in Iraq. The reasons for Blair's commitment to these policies are difficult to assess with any accuracy so close to the events.

- **The world leader** – this view of Blair is closely associated with the 'war leader' argument and is summarised efficiently by Tony Judt, Professor of European Studies at New York University:

Tony Blair is an extremely interesting man. He is a man with a set of beliefs about how the world ought to look, how the world needs to be run if it is to remain at peace with itself, if poverty is to be addressed, if disease and environmental difficulties are to be addressed. So he has a world picture, which makes him unusual for most politicians who think much more locally and short term.[8]

- **The man of moral certainty** – this is similar to the 'air of certainty' discussed above yet has a stronger resonance since 2001. Chris Smith, Blair's Culture Minister from the first government, attempted to define this aspect of Blair's character: 'There are moments certainly in the past few years when, in terms of foreign policy, Blair has identified something that he really passionately believes as a moral purpose. And he's determined, even if it means standing alone against the rest of the world, that he's going to try and pursue that . . . I think there's a little bit of that that has come through in relation to Iraq. He has always seen this as something that he believes in. He believes in the rightness of the cause, and even though a lot of the world around him was saying, 'No, this is the wrong thing to be doing,' he nonetheless thought, 'I think I'm right and I'm going to stick by it'. It's what he's done in the past and I think he thought that, having been proved right in the past, he would be proved right on this as well . . .'[9]
- **The aloof leader** – this criticism of the Blair style of government since 2001 has been discussed at length by a number of observers, most notably in the 2004 Butler Report on the Review of Intelligence on Weapons of Mass Destruction, that criticised the Blair style of informal government and an overdependency on political advisers. Government spokespersons dismissed Butler's findings on the grounds that good government was about results, not style. The earlier Hutton Report, however, while exonerating Blair from most of the accusations levelled at the government, revealed much about a political style that had indeed become 'aloof'.
- **The beleaguered leader** – this is where we observe Blair genuinely 'tested by crises' in the way that Kavanagh thought would define him as a leader in 2001. There are three distinct periods in which Blair has had to handle immense pressure. The experience of this has certainly done much to change his physical appearance and has also done much to frame what may well be our lasting perceptions of his political style. The first of these periods may be defined as that period between late summer 2003 and January

2004 when the suicide of the weapons inspector, Dr David Kelly, led to the Hutton Inquiry. The week of the publication coincided with a less than certain vote in the House of Commons on top-up fees. The second key period we may highlight is the 2005 general election when all the public unrest about continued involvement in Iraq and specifically about the trust and integrity of Blair himself became key election issues. Finally, the extraordinary events of the second week in July 2005 showed Blair in all the possible stages of emotion linked to the post of Prime Minister. At the start of the week, London hosted the Live 8 concert designed to put pressure on the G8 leaders, when they met in Gleneagles a few days later, to solve the issue of world poverty, particularly in Africa. On the Tuesday of that week, Blair flew to Singapore to be part of the final push in what turned out to be London's successful bid to host the 2012 Olympic Games before flying back to Scotland to host the G8 meeting. On Thursday, 7 July, a series of terrorist bombs exploded on the London transport network. Ben Macintyre, writing in *The Times* (9 July 2005) said that: 'For months Tony Blair has plotted and fretted over his legacy, only to have his historical inheritance set in stone in one tumultuous 24-hour period.' Even at his most stretched and beleaguered, however, the Blair skills of rhetoric and language were once again evident as he spoke first at the Gleneagles G8 summit and then again later in London. This tumultuous week showed the Blair style of leadership in almost every facet of its range.

Having looked at the leadership style of Tony Blair, we can go on to compare it with that of Margaret Thatcher, the Prime Minister probably most often compared with Blair.

The case of Margaret Thatcher: not 'to be' but 'to do'

Thatcher was without doubt the most dominant peacetime Prime Minister of the twentieth century. There are many aspects of her leadership style that bear close comparison with Tony Blair. These include:

- The outsider in the party.
- Willingness to shift significantly from the 'old' party ideology.

- Dominated Cabinet and willing to be seen apart from it.
- Willingness to lead from the centre as head of a highly personalised government.
- Effective use of 'hiding' and giving a sense of distance from government when it suited.
- Conviction and moral certainty of a personal political message as opposed to collegiality and consensus.

Thatcher's style may be defined in relation to a turning point in her time in power in a similar way to that outlined above for Blair. Having won the general election in 1979, Thatcher found herself as head of a Conservative government that, unlike Blair's experience in 1997, still contained many of the old Tory 'grandees', and a very high level of unpopularity in the country. By the end of 1981, Thatcher faced a worsening situation that included rising unemployment and inflation, a range of serious economic problems and a Cabinet which was very much split on how best to manage the government. We should highlight three developments that saved Thatcher from what appeared to be certain electoral defeat when viewed from the perspective of early 1982.

- **The Falklands War** – where Argentina misread British intentions towards possession of the Falkland Islands in the South Atlantic and subsequently invaded. Thatcher's response was to send a task force to the South Atlantic to take back control of the islands and restore British sovereignty in the process. The campaign was daring and audacious, and the potential for military disaster at the end of a very long supply line was considerable. British forces finally recovered the islands, however, in the face of patchy resistance from ill-armed and ill-trained Argentinian forces. There was loss of life on both sides, most notably in set-piece attacks on shipping, including the Argentinian *General Belgrano* and the British ships, HMS *Sheffield* and *Sir Galahad*, among others. Thatcher's reputation was made by the Falklands war in the way that Blair's was tarnished by the war in Iraq. For both leaders, the future became filtered through the events of war. Thatcher became a tabloid heroine (as opposed to the demonisation of Blair, especially in the *Daily Mirror*), and the Conservatives went on to win an election in 1983 that looked very much beyond them in late 1981.

This was the key turning point in the consolidation of Thatcher's premiership and reveals much about her leadership style.

- **Sacking the 'wets'** – the 'wets' were those members of the Cabinet between 1979 and 1982 who were not in favour of Thatcher's policies and who actively opposed them. Thatcher moved against the wets – Jim Prior, Ian Gilmour, Peter Walker – and established a domination over the Cabinet that would not be challenged until the late 1980s. Once again, the tabloid version of these events framed Thatcher as determined and focused rather than tyrannical and antidemocratic.

- **The economy** – began to recover. High levels of unemployment associated with the government's economic policies began to fall and the high levels of inflation associated with the government also began to fall. While these developments owed little to the political skill of Thatcher, her handling of economic issues certainly added to the media and popular perception of her as someone determined to 'have her way' with the direction and policy of the government.

Thatcher won three consecutive election victories – 1979, 1983 and 1987. Her grip on the Conservative Party began to weaken around the late 1980s and was characterised by her flawed decision to introduce the Poll Tax and her growing resistance to Britain's place in the European Union. More long-term observations of her decline also point to the 1985–6 Westland Helicopters dispute as a point beyond which Thatcher began to attract the deep-seated resentment in the party that would eventually result in her being challenged for the leadership by Michael Heseltine in 1990. Although the party declined to elect Heseltine in her place, Thatcher's career as Prime Minister was over and she was replaced by John Major, more of whom later.

Thatcher's political and leadership style has been much debated. Here, we can attempt to draw together some of the defining elements of this style in terms of the impact that it had on the workings of the political system in Britain. In short, Thatcher's leadership style:

- Reduced the number of cabinet meetings and cut down on paperwork. This trend would be accelerated under Blair.
- Made greater use of the kitchen cabinet and *ad hoc* committees.
- Allowed intervention in departmental affairs.

Box 7.2 Thatcher's and Blair's advantages: a comparison

Thatcher	Blair
Her extended tenure in office meant that, by the 1980s, many holders of senior posts in public service had been appointed by her and, in a sense, 'owed' her	Blair may be approaching a similar situation. The press is certainly fond of regular periods of criticism over 'Blair's cronies'
Consistently large Commons majorities	Blair has formed three governments based on large majorities. Even the significant dip in support for the Labour Party in 2005 gave Blair a larger majority than that enjoyed by Thatcher in 1979 and Major in 1992
Determined and forthright personality – did not suffer fools or opposition gladly	Blair has a similar approach and personality, albeit less direct and confrontational than Thatcher
Widespread public support	Blair continues to enjoy public support (even though the 2005 general election saw a government returned with a small proportion of the popular vote and a decline in his personal popularity ratings)
Highly respected abroad	Blair has almost outdone Thatcher on this one. Playing a key role in the 'war on terrorism' and attempting to play a pivotal role in the EU
A sense of vision	Less strident and direct than Thatcher, but no less convinced of his sense of duty, moral certainty and conviction
Weak parliamentary opposition	The Conservative opposition to Blair has been almost as disorganised and disjointed as the Labour opposition to Thatcher was throughout the 1980s

- Showed the workings of an odd relationship with the convention of collective cabinet responsibility. Thatcher was prepared to leak and brief against ministers when it suited her but, in turn, was equally forceful in demanding adherence to the same doctrine from her ministers.
- Showed a preparedness to make major policy decisions without first consulting Cabinet and to keep some major issues off the cabinet agenda altogether. Examples include support for the American bombing of Libya in 1986 and excluding trade unions from organising in the Government Communications Headquarters at Cheltenham in 1984. Michael Heseltine would also claim this as the main reason for his resignation from the Cabinet in 1986.
- Showed a willingness to appoint weak ministers who could then be easily controlled.
- Had a distinct approach to cabinet meetings that would begin with her stating her own views. Major took the more conventional approach of listening first, then summing up at the end.
- Represented a populist appeal to those who had come to feel marginalised by the 1970s and developed a style that was highly substantive in content and directly confrontational in approach.

The extent to which Thatcher's style has been responsible for permanent changes to the nature of central government has also been debated in detail. Thatcher's period in office has been synonymous with discussions on the gradual presidentialism of the office of Prime Minister, yet many writers argue that Thatcher had advantages at her disposal that other holders of the office did not, and that many of Thatcher's strengths were not permanent. McNaughton's view of Thatcher's advantages are summarised in the box below:[10]

McNaughton goes on to make the point that, in relation to the factors we have highlighted in the table, these all work essentially in the short term. As Kavanagh has pointed out, however, what were initially considered to be Thatcher's strengths and assets were far from permanent. We have already outlined how, by 1900, Thatcher had lost the confidence of many in her Cabinet and her once instinctive connection with the mass of the electorate had all but evaporated. It remains to be seen how many of the factors we have compared against Blair in Box 7.2 will also disappear, or if Blair will indeed use his pre-announced retirement from the post to cheat a particular judgement of history.

The case of John Major: the 'poor general'

During the Live 8 campaign in the summer of 2005, the former Conservative Prime Minister, John Major, revealed in an interview that he regretted not doing enough for Africa during his time in office (1990–7). It is this type of reflection, taken alongside his record of government, that does nothing to distract from the generally held view of the Major style of leadership and politics as one of basic failure and disappointment. The complete history of the Major years has yet to be written yet we can begin to offer an overview of assessments of his leadership style and to make some significant comparisons with both Thatcher and Blair.

According to Foley, Major's problems as Prime Minister stemmed from the circumstances of his accession to office. In the shadow of Thatcher's confrontational and intransigent attitude (especially over the issue of Europe) Major had been the consensus candidate for the leadership of the Conservative Party. Following the shell-burst of Thatcherism, Major represented the 'fair minded integrity and civil service attributes of being able to assimilate contrasting positions within a single brief that allowed him to preside through ambiguity and nuance' (Foley). In quoting Allan Massie of the *Daily Telegraph* of August 1993, however, even after her departure, the tensions implicit in Thatcher's removal had not been resolved and it was because of this impasse that 'Major's position became so problematic'. As Massie concluded, 'few Prime Ministers have had their leadership qualities so persistently questioned'. There were still almost four years of the Major premiership remaining and, as Foley points out, 'What was true in 1993 remained equally valid for the remainder of Major's premiership'. This was made even more difficult by Major clearly not being Thatcher in a party that had got used to the Thatcher style, and by the existence of a subgroup among the Conservatives which, disciple-like, attempted to continue pushing the Thatcherite agenda and opposing any attempt to dilute the political message of their lost leader.

What you should have learnt from reading this chapter

Leadership style is an important factor in the success or failure of any Prime Minister, and this chapter has outlined why this is the case. It is important to remember, however, that the style of a Prime Minister should not become the main focus of study. Leadership style becomes truly significant only when measured alongside political structures and the wider political contexts.

Glossary of key terms

Balancer A prime ministerial style as identified by Norton. The balancer seeks stability in his or her party and in society as a whole.

Egoist Another prime ministerial style identified by Norton. For the egoist, political power is an end in itself. The egoist seeks to gain power and then to retain and exercise that power for as long as possible.

Innovator Norton again: for the innovator, power is the means by which some future goal may be achieved. Most innovators are driven by some degree of ideological motivation.

Personality The personal characteristics and character traits of the Prime Minister.

Reformer Norton's fourth prime ministerial style: the reformer seeks to achieve power in order to deliver a future goal.

Style The distinct approach to the position of Prime Minister by its holder, conditioned to an extent by personality.

Likely examination questions

Short questions

Explain why 'style' is important in studies of the Prime Minister.

Summarise Norton's four fold typology of prime ministerial styles.

Briefly compare the political and leadership styles of Margaret Thatcher, John Major and Tony Blair.

Essay questions

'The style of the Prime Minister is largely determined by his or her party.' To what extent do you agree?

To what extent is style the most important factor to consider when assessing a Prime Minister?

How far would you agree with the claim that Blair's style sets him apart from other post-war Prime Ministers?

Discuss the importance of prime ministerial style.

Revision task

Research the political style of Tony Blair and produce a 'style profile' that shows his similarities and differences with other recent Prime Ministers.

Helpful websites

www.number10.gov.uk/

www.direct.gov.uk/

www.cabinetoffice.gov.uk/

Suggestions for further reading

Fairclough, N. (2000) *New Labour, New Language?* (Routledge).

Foley, M. (2000) *The British Presidency* (Manchester University Press).

Foley, M. (2002) *Major, Blair and a Conflict of Leadership: Collision Course* (Manchester University Press).

Heywood, A. (1997) *Politics* (Macmillan).

Kampfner, J. (2003) *Blair's Wars* (Free Press).

Kavanagh, D. (2001) 'Blair as Prime Minister', *Politics Review*, vol. 11.1, September 2001.

Mandelson, P. and Liddle, R. (1996) *The Blair Revolution* (Politico's).

McNaughton, N. (1999) *The Prime Minister and Cabinet Government* (Hodder).

Norton, P. (1987) 'Prime ministerial Power: Framework for Analysis', *Teaching Politics*, vol. 16.3, September 1987.

Rentoul, J. (2001) *Tony Blair: Prime Minister* (Time Warner).

Rose, R. (2001) *The Prime Minister in a Shrinking World* (Polity Press).

Seldon, A. (2004) *Blair* (Free Press).

The Prime Minister: Hail to the Chief?

Contents

Overview

This chapter will address the key question – to what extent does a British 'President' now occupy Number 10 Downing Street? The question acknowledges the dissatisfaction with two earlier claims. The first being that the British system of government is largely organised around the collective decisions of the Cabinet, while the second claims that collective government by the Cabinet has been replaced by prime ministerial government. To argue that the Prime Minister is now a President is to move the debate on and to claim that what we are now able to observe comprises features in the powers of the Prime Minister that make him/her look more like a European- or American-type President.

Key issues to be covered in this chapter

- An overview of the debate surrounding the issue of prime ministerial versus presidential government
- We shall recap on the growing power of the British Prime Minister and provide examples from the prime ministerial careers of Margaret Thatcher and Tony Blair
- The arguments for and against presidentialism will be outlined, as will the key arguments of Michael Foley.

Introduction

It cannot be a coincidence that the debate surrounding the powers of the Prime Minister should be at its most invigorating when a leader with a degree of charisma and a sizeable Commons majority occupies the post. Harold Wilson after 1964, Margaret Thatcher for most of the 1980s, and Tony Blair since 1997 – all have governed with distinctive styles and approaches that encourage reappraisals of those powers held by the Prime Minister. In the previous chapters, we set out the roles and powers of the Prime Minister and highlighted the sources of this prime ministerial power. We also recapped on the somewhat 'loose' nature of constitutional restraint on these powers. These are issues worth keeping in mind when entering the 'Prime Minister versus President' debate.

The growing powers of the Prime Minister

It is difficult to argue against the claim that the British Prime Minister now has at his or her disposal more power than was the case in the immediate post-war era, and that these powers are both consequence and cause of the changing nature of the British cabinet system.

The basic powers of the Prime Minister, which have evolved since the late eighteenth century, are fundamentally the same as they ever were. What has changed, however, is the nature of the exercise of these powers and, in particular, the increased concentration of power in the office of the Prime Minister and subsequent 'systems of personal rule', as highlighted by critics of these developments. The arena in which these powers are exercised has also changed dramatically and has had a huge impact on the role of the Prime Minister. These changes may be summarised as:

- The development of increasingly complex government machinery.
- Mass and near-instant global communication.
- The impact of the internet and the world wide web.
- A largely media-driven public interaction with politics.
- A growing sense of apathy and disengagement among the electorate.
- The general decline in ideology-based politics.
- The end of the Cold War.

- The rise to power of an entirely post-war political establishment.
- A relatively stable economy.

These are all changes and developments that point to a 'new' kind of politics that the office of the Prime Minister has had to evolve alongside. The questions relating to prime ministerial power have been debated since the 1960s and are particularly relevant when applied to Blair. In seeking to examine the 'Prime Minister/President', issue it may by useful to begin the discussion by setting out exactly what it is we mean when we use the phrase 'prime ministerial government'

Prime ministerial government

For a system to be described as **prime ministerial**, there are eight key features that need to be present. The Prime Minister:

- Dominates the policy-making process.
- Takes responsibility for all key policy decisions.
- Will dominate the Cabinet.
- Will determine the outcome of the process of collective responsibility.
- Will claim a separate source of authority from party and electorate and not rely exclusively on Parliament.
- Will act as the principal spokesperson for the government and will be treated as the ultimate interpreter of government policy.
- Will clear all key decisions made by cabinet ministers.
- Will make good use of prerogative powers that allow him or her to act as head of state. This is especially relevant to foreign policy, defence and security which tend to be personal powers of the Prime Minister and subject to few controls.

To develop this further, Moran offers a straightforward set of points in favour and against the suggestion that prime ministerial government now exists. These are summarised in Table 8.1.[1]

When they begin to question whether prime ministerial government still exists, other writers tend to distinguish between the short-term factors which determine how dominant the individual office holder is, and the long-term factors which may lead to the office itself (whoever holds it) becoming more important. It will be useful to have

Table 8.1 Evidence for and against prime ministerial government

Evidence FOR	Evidence AGAINST
• The value of prime ministerial patronage. • Prime Minister chooses ministers. • Prime Minister now dominates modern elections. • Prime Ministers can attempt to exercise influence across all of government, not just a department. • The Prime Minister is now the key figure in ensuring 'joined-up' government. • The Prime Minister is the key figurehead of government.	• Patronage is too vast – appointments can be made only on the advice of others. • There are always rivals in Cabinet. • If the next election victory is in doubt, a Prime Minister will not be able to control all of the Cabinet. • The resources available to a Prime Minister for him/her to attempt to oversee all government are few. • World events may be dramatic yet can become troublesome and allow a rival to hijack the domestic agenda.

an overview of the positions of writers, such as Seldon and Hennessy,[2] in relation to these long-and short-term factors.

Short-term factors

• **The size of the parliamentary majority** provides a sense of security and allows domination of Parliament. It also imparts huge personal authority. Blair's two huge majorities and Thatcher's wins in 1983 and 1987 gave both leaders a big advantage. Jim Callaghan and John Major were less fortunate and therefore appeared weak.

• **The state of the ruling party** can make opposition seem insignificant if the party is united. To challenge the Prime Minister, ambitious colleagues need some degree of dissent in the party. Blair's cabinets have been largely compliant. In contrast, between 1979 and 1982, Thatcher had major problems with important factions in the party. Only her personal stature and victory in the Falklands War enabled her to triumph.

- **The personal popularity of the leader** is a very important factor. Until the war in Iraq began to have a serious impact on his personal ratings, Blair enjoyed this particular advantage up to 2001/2 (and may do so again) whilst Thatcher enjoyed high levels of popularity from across significantly large cross-sections of classes in Britain.

- **Events and luck** – factors no Prime Minister can truly claim to control. For most of the time, Blair has been a 'lucky' Prime Minister. Labour inherited a mostly robust economy that has continued to remain stable, and he has faced a Conservative Party that has had major problems reinventing itself. His foreign and diplomatic policies, however, have been a mixed blessings. Initial successes in Northern Ireland and a clear 'moral' leadership in the Balkans were topped by a masterly political performance in the immediate aftermath of the 11 September attacks. His policy towards Iraq and the 'war on terrorism' have, however, had negative effects on his personal ratings, and have made it difficult for him to re-establish a clear domestic agenda. The terrorist attacks on London in July 2005 allowed Blair to play to his strengths as a national leader, however. By comparison, after 1991, Major staggered from one policy disaster to another whereas Thatcher enjoyed substantial 'luck' at a critical point in her premiership in the form of the Falklands War.

It is important to note that none of the factors discussed here is what we could describe as 'permanent'. They may, indeed, have an impact on the standing and style of a Prime Minister, yet remain, as we have shown, short term and therefore difficult to build into the key debate.

To get to a closer understanding of what constitutes prime ministerial government, we need to examine the long-term factors that may have brought about permanent changes in how a Prime Minister governs. McNaugton suggests there are five of these factors to consider:[3]

- **The marginalisation of the Cabinet**. This is a theme we have already discussed at length. To what extent has the nature of the relationship between the Cabinet and the Prime Minister changed? To what extent is the Cabinet still the arena for the major policy decisions? Critics of prime ministerial power point to short and infrequent meetings as just two examples from many that illustrate the reduced circumstances of cabinet government in Britain.

- **Media and public perceptions**. The key point to make here is that the public, the media, pressure groups and the wider political community, Parliament and Whitehall, have fundamentally changed their perceptions of the Prime Minister. The body of evidence is growing – especially the data collected from focus groups and opinion polls – that the Prime Minister is increasingly looked upon as the single representative of the government as a whole and, in some cases, of the state. In other words, as a President.

- **Institutional changes**. These changes are most likely to include changes and reforms to the central government machinery and administration. We have already made a case for the changed role of the Cabinet Office and the example fits this factor particularly well. We have noted that the size of the Cabinet Office has doubled under Blair, and that it has become much more of a personal resource for the Prime Minister rather than for the Cabinet. We have also discussed at length the increased use of specialist and personal advisers. Here again, we have evidence of significant and permanent institutional changes that appear to give major advantages to the Prime Minister.

- **External factors**. This argument revisits the Richard Rose theory outlined in Chapter 5. Closer integration with the European Union may well have placed the Prime Minister more firmly at the centre of foreign relations. Similarly, Britain's increased role in world affairs has thrust the Prime Minister increasingly into the limelight of the world's media. This is particularly relevant to Tony Blair who has had a higher foreign profile than most recent Prime Ministers.

- **Constitutional changes**. As far as Blair is concerned, this may be one area, on paper at least, where the New Labour reforms have actually reduced the influence of the Prime Minister. Devolution has certainly removed some power from central government, while the enhanced authority of the reformed House of Lords has caused parliamentary difficulties for Blair.

Having established a broad definition of prime ministerial government, it will be useful to do something similar with the concept of presidential government.

Presidential government

Nigel Jackson offers a starting point for this discussion by listing seven key factors that could currently be used to support the presidential government debate.[4] According to Jackson, the Prime Minister:

- Is becoming more detached from government, Parliament and the party organisation.
- Increasingly assumes a 'detached' role as the leader of the nation.
- Has significantly increased the Number 10 staff in recent years.
- Has downgraded cabinet meetings and cabinet government in general.
- Has increased his/her 'control style'.
- Has contributed to the politicisation of the Civil Service.
- Shows a preference for taking decisions alone or in bilateral meetings.

Jackson argues that the last five of these factors have an increased significance when applied to Blair.

It is inevitable that the use of the word 'President' in this context invites direct comparison with the American system rather than with any general notion of presidential government. It will therefore be useful to have a checklist of key strengths of the American President to compare with the current position of the British Prime Minister. There are six key strengths enjoyed by the American President that we could summarise here.

Contrasts between Presidential & Prime Ministerial

- The President is elected directly by the people, and authority is drawn from the people.
- It is not necessary for the President to depend upon the constant support of the legislature to survive in office. The President can afford to be defeated in Congress yet will not be expected to resign.
- The President is head of state and head of government, and can play the roles against each other, especially in appeals directly to the electorate. Here, the President can claim to represent the

nation as a whole while other government leaders are seen as partisan politicians who operate only for partisan interests.

- Over 4,000 officials are appointed by the President at the start of the administration, this represents enormous powers of patronage.
- A far greater bureaucracy than that available to the British Prime Minister supports the President.
- The American media allow the President direct access and can be used on demand to speak to and for the nation.

Similar to the constraints on prime ministerial power outlined earlier, it is important to note three significant restrictions on the powers of the American President. These include working under a **strict Constitution** as part of a system of **checks and balances** in a **fixed term** of four years restricted to two terms in office.

Comparing the Prime Minister and the President

When we compare the respective powers and strengths of the President of the United States and the British Prime Minister, it becomes clear that there are similarities and differences (see Box 8.1). The holders of both offices clearly enjoy substantial powers of patronage, control of the media, policy-making support and the ability/tendency to act as a national leader. The President is officially head of state, however, and can claim direct authority from the people, he or she will not be removed from office other than for misconduct. The Prime Minister, on the other hand, does not operate under the same built-in political checks as the President nor does the British system bind the Prime Minister within a rigid set of constitutional constraints. Therefore, based on a simple UK/US comparison, it would appear that there are several almost 'permanent' differences that prevent the British Prime Minister becoming an American-style president, yet the debate remains. The focus of this chapter can now switch to a detailed examination of this debate.

President or Prime Minister? The debate

With its modern origins in discussions of Thatcher's political style from 1979 to 1990, this is not a new debate. By the end of her time

Box 8.1 Comparison of the Prime Minister and the President

Similarities	Differences
• More Patronage	• President is also the head of state
• Better use of the media	• President has authority directly from the people
• More policy-making support	• President cannot be moved from the legislature except for misconduct
• Tendency to appear as the national leader	• President's popularity does not depend on support of his or her party
	• President has to work with in-built political checks
	• President operates within constitutional constraints

in power, Thatcher had sacked a lot of ministers, and an equally large number had felt the need to resign. The memoirs and autobiographies of many former ministers were highly critical of the Thatcher style. The sacked and the reshuffled contributed to a first draft of history mostly as critics of a method of government that had subverted collective cabinet decision-making. This testimony is flawed on the grounds that 'they would say that, wouldn't they?' The dismissals of James Prior and Ian Gilmour, and the resignations of Heseltine, Howe and Lawson were rancorous and bitter affairs, and the last act of 'revenge' lay ultimately in the pens of these fallen ministers. In this debate, the point to stress about Thatcher is that the style of leadership may have been more striking than the substance of any real institutional change. As we have already stressed elsewhere, especially in Chapter 7, the style of the Prime Minister is an important factor that cannot be overlooked. The debate on this particular issue is rich and lively, and we cannot hope to present all the various theories and competing arguments here but can offer a succinct overview of the crucial writers and their opinions. These will include Burch, Jones, Johnson,

Kavanagh and Seldon, and Hennessy. Particular attention will be paid to the work of Michael Foley.

Peter Hennessy[5]

Hennessy is cautious in his discussion of the power of the Prime Minister, and he does not believe we should make the assumption that this power will inevitably increase and that we are observing a permanent move from prime ministerial to presidential government. For writers like Hennessy, the office of Prime Minister is essentially flexible and malleable and will be shaped by individual premiers according to how he or she wishes. Occasionally, these changes look so dramatic that observers jump to the conclusion that they must therefore be permanent. This is simply not the case; there will always be forces at work in the British political system that will prevent any Prime Minister from establishing complete dominance over it.

In his most recent study, Hennessy does not seek to deny that, in Thatcher and Blair, we have witnessed two 'remarkable' holders of the office who have succeeded in stretching the potential of that office about as far as it will go. Thatcher and Blair have been 'commanders' of the system, with decisive leadership styles that have inevitably been described as 'presidential'. Does this therefore mean that the office of Prime Minister has changed fundamentally? Hennessy thinks that this is not the case. He makes several points to support his argument:

- Strong and dominant leaders are nothing new. Peel, Gladstone, Lloyd George and Churchill all dominated the system. The system has also had periods, however, where it has 'relaxed' during the terms of Prime Ministers such as John Major.
- Britain is a constitutional monarchy, and we shouldn't forget it. The Prime Minister is not the head of state and can never entirely rely on the absolute loyalty of the political community.
- Britain is also a parliamentary democracy. Political authority flows through Parliament and, as long as it does so, that body will exercise ultimate control over prime ministerial power.
- Finally, Britain remains an open, pluralist society. The highly centralised 'command model' of prime ministerial government does not, therefore, accord with the nature of the political culture. For Hennessy, power is an extremely diffuse concept and cannot be

readily captured by the holder of one office on a long-term basis. We should therefore guard against the easy temptation to accept that the current trends in prime ministerial government are permanent.

Martin Burch[6]

Burch is also sceptical about the notion of a presidential Prime Minister even though his 1990 study is restricted to an analysis of Thatcher. His conclusions remain valid nevertheless. In a way similar to Hennessy, he notes that there are practical restrictions on the Prime Minister's formal power to hire and fire ministers, there are limits on the involvement of a Prime Minister in the initiation of policy; and there are constraints on the capacity of the Prime Minister to control government business.

George Jones[7]

Again, the two studies by Jones considerably predate Blair. His conclusions remain significant in their analysis of Thatcher, hpwever. Jones is similar to Hennessy in that he does not necessarily believe that the changes to prime ministerial power are permanent. He uses the metaphor of an elastic band to illustrate his argument that a Prime Minister may stretch the powers of the office well beyond that which would usually be considered 'normal'. In the same way that an elastic band stretched to its limits will exhibit considerable tensions to return to an unstretched state, however, then so the powers of the Prime Minister when distorted by individuals, such as Margaret Thatcher, will naturally seek to 'snap back'. When the band 'snapped back' on Thatcher in 1990, it was forceful enough to remove her from office. How much tension is the elastic band under during Blair's third administration? Jones concedes that Prime Ministers can be in a powerful position, but only so long as they can carry their colleagues with them – they are only as strong as their colleagues allow them to be. The theory is underlined by the position of John Major who suffered from a small parliamentary majority, a divided party and a press that branded him as weak and dithering. It is worth noting that the Major premiership caused the debate on the 'presidential' Prime Minister to subside until Blair took power on the back of a huge majority and a lively and energetic leadership style.

Dennis Kavanagh[8]

We spoke earlier of the 'long-term' factors that have brought about permanent changes in the way the Prime Minister exercises power. In Seldon's *The Blair Effect* Kavanagh, saw Blair as early as 2000 as having already made a long-term impact on the office of Prime Minister. He sees Blair as a leader who has demanded a reanimation of the office in a way that would have an impact the length and breadth of Whitehall. Kavanagh also argues that Blair has set the bar for his successors to the extent that they are likely to wish to emulate a number of his practices. Some of the practices used by Blair may well be part of a long-term trend but some are new.

Blair's impact will be permanent. He will leave his mark to a greater extent than other powerful Prime Ministers who came before him. Lloyd George, for instance, created the Cabinet Office and the system of cabinet committees, and they strengthened his position. The innovations, however, did not survive him. Even Thatcher, with her new style of dominant leadership, left little lasting effect, as the whole basis of her approach was constructed around her own personality. When she went, then so did the façade of her style, and it was impossible to hand such a thing to any successor, whoever that may have been. Kavanagh believes that Blair's impact will be permanent for two main reasons:

- The Cabinet Office and the Prime Minister's Private Office have seen a dramatic growth under Blair. As we have already noted, Blair has a Prime Minister's Department, all that is missing is the formal title. The Policy Unit has grown, special advisers recruited and a whole plethora of units and commissions has been hitched to Number 10 in a confusing and Byzantine manner. The point is, all of them report to Blair as Prime Minister. He now has a wide range of individuals and bodies that feed policy advice to him. Where does this leave the Cabinet?
- There has been a major change in Blair's relationship with other bodies in the political centre. The party is no longer as important as it once was, and Blair has shown how effectively a leader can control his own party. The importance of Parliament in the system, especially the Commons, has declined while the Cabinet is seen as a body of subordinates rather than as political colleagues. Only

Gordon Brown and his team at the Treasury give Blair pause for thought in this respect. Finally the Civil Service has been brought under control. Special advisers have had an impact here alongside Blair's determination to influence senior appointments.

To summarise the two points being made by Kavanagh: the traditional limitations of prime ministerial power have declined.

As far as the future is concerned, Kavanagh believes that Blair's 'system' will last. It is highly unlikely that successors will dismantle a system designed to give the Prime Minister so much dominance, and it will therefore endure. Blair has, concludes Kavanagh, fashioned a stronger role for the Prime Minister in the British system, and that this has been due partly to his own ideas about effective political leadership and partly by trends in politics and media coverage. On a final note of caution, Kavanagh reminds us of the potential for hubris associated with such power. As the Prime Minister becomes increasingly separated from the Cabinet, the ruling party and Parliament, it will be the Prime Minister who will be left shouldering the blame if things go wrong. The greater the Prime Minister, the greater the final fall from grace. If this happens to Blair, it will not be a unique event and will stand alongside the downfall of Thatcher in 1990 as an example of the down side of such concentration of power.

Michael Foley[9]

Foley's initial analysis is again dominated by Thatcher, although his first study, published in 1994, was updated in much more detail in 2000 with the publication of *The British Presidency* which focuses in great detail on Blair and the 'politics of public leadership'.

In his original analysis, Foley has argued that some features of the American presidency may be employed to analyse some of the changes in the role of the Prime Minister which have taken place since the late 1970s. He isolates four features of the American presidency which, he claims, have been adopted by British Prime Ministers. We will summarise these four features in Box 8.2:

Blair fits neatly into this analysis:

- Spatial leadership was displayed early in his career as Prime Minister when he distanced himself from political corruption by Labour MPs and some Labour councils. Both were quickly

Box 8.2 Michael Foley on the British presidency (1994)

Spatial leadership
This term refers to the attempts made by American Presidents to distance themselves politically from the presidency when it is expedient to do so. Foley uses Major's Citizen's Charter as a good example of the way in which this idea has been adopted in the UK. By publicly criticising bureaucratic elements of government, Major gave the impression that he was on the side of the ordinary citizen, battling against oppressive bureaucracy.

Public leadership
This particular aspect of the thesis is best seen when the President/Prime Minister appeals for support directly over the head of Congress/Parliament. Foley argues that television has become crucial to this, and has allowed the leader to devep a relationship with the public that is now central and decisive.

Cult of the outsider
This is the distance claimed by either President or Prime Minister from the political establishment. Nixon, Carter, Reagan and Clinton in the United States, and every British Prime Minister since Callaghan have claimed to be outsiders and therefore not to have the vested interest of the government insider. Thatcher was particularly adept at this in the way she courted the rank and file of her party and dealt in populist politics that circumvented party élites and Whitehall.

The personal factor
In both the United States and Britain an integrated image of a party and its programme is now being routed through its leader. In this way, differences between parties tend to become personalised. It is assumed that the personal qualities of the Prime Minister and other leaders are central to public evaluations of political leadership and performance.

disowned before any case had been proved against anyone involved. He has also shown similar inclinations in his dealings with the trade union movement and other symbols of Labour's socialist past.

- Blair has never been anything else than an outsider in the party he leads. He has no family connection and served no student apprenticeship in the Labour Party. His attitude to Labour's history and to sacred cows, such as Clause IV, provides further evidence of this tendency. The success of this approach has been carried through into government.

- In terms of public leadership and the use of the media, Blair, the consummate actor, provides us with countless examples of his astute handling of the modern media. His speeches on the death of Princess Diana and his responses to terrorist attacks in New York and London showed a clear skill in projecting himself as the national expression of popular concern and the public interest.
- Blair has also made much of his personal qualities – youth (relatively, in 1997), family man, 'decent', moral and clearly Christian.

Foley also uses the American President, Ronald Reagan, as well as Margaret Thatcher to illustrate his arguments, particularly on spatial leadership. Reagan was able to place himself 'outside' the system when Congress attempted to push through unpopular policies, while Thatcher's credentials as a true political 'outsider' were even more noticeable.

Foley is attempting here to cut us away from the old debate about cabinet versus prime ministerial government. To replace this idea, he is asking us to consider the possibility that something completely new is evolving.

If the modern Prime Minister is indeed 'separate' from his/her Cabinet, it does not imply a 'dominance' of Cabinet, or a simple shift in the balance of power. This is a brand-new style of leadership.

We have returned to our earlier distinctions regarding the substance of style. The British Prime Minister may now exhibit a political style of leadership that looks essentially presidential, but this does not mean that the British Prime Minister is becoming an American-style president. The constitutional differences between Britain and the United States are too great for that. Rather, Foley suggests: 'The British Prime Minister has, to all intent and purposes, turned, not into a British version of the American President, but into an authentically British President.'

••

✔ What you should have learnt from reading this chapter

This chapter has outlined several of the essential debates relevant to the discussion of the 'presidentialism' of the British Prime Minister.

This is a very complex and fluid debate. This chapter has provided only an overview of the essential arguments. Wider reading here is important to gain a more detailed understanding. Foley, in particular, is a 'must read'.

The debate can often appear simplistic, especially when straightforward comparisons are made between the British Prime Minister and the American President. In many ways, such a comparison is meaningless, given the very different natures of the two systems of government. Instead, we would do well to come away from this debate with the recognition that there is clearly a process of change taking place that may well be producing a British 'President' but not an 'American British President'.

The future of prime ministerial styles beyond Blair will obviously add much to this discussion. Will the system post-Blair be as fundamentally changed as writers like Kavanagh have suggested, or will the more cautious views of Hennessy, Burch and Jones be played out in a move away from prime ministerial government? Or will a Gordon Brown (or whoever) premiership slip neatly into the new and successful leadership style as outlined by Foley?

Glossary of key terms

Presidentialism The process some observers claim to detect in the evolution of the British Prime Minister into something approaching an American-style president.

Prime ministerial government The system of government with a directly elected individual as head of government.

Spatial leadership This term refers to the attempts made by American Presidents to distance themselves politically from the presidency when it is expedient to do so.

Likely examination questions

Short questions

Explain the essential features of presidential government.

Explain the essential details of prime ministerial government.

Briefly explain the concept of spatial leadership.

Essay questions

'Tony Blair is a President.' Discuss.

How far would you agree with the suggestion that the Prime Minister has presidential-type powers?

'A British President is not a welcome development.' Discuss.

Revision tasks

Monitor the news for two weeks. Make a list of actions carried out by the British Prime Minister and the American President. How many of the actions carried out by one could equally be carried out by the other? Plot your findings on an 'example table' and be sure to explain your judgements.

Design and produce a revision chart that shows the key arguments surrounding the 'Prime Minister as President' debate.

Helpful websites

www.number10.gov.uk/

www.direct.gov.uk/

www.cabinetoffice.gov.uk/

http://news.bbc.co.uk

The BBC website is particularly good for tracking the various changes in central government.

http://politics.guardian.co.uk

An excellent website for political analysis and for tracking this particular debate.

www.whitehouse.gov/WH/EOP

For American comparisons.

Suggestions for further reading

Foley, M. (2000) *The British Presidency* (Manchester University Press).

Foley, M. (2002) *Major, Blair and a Conflict of Leadership*: *Collision Course* (Manchester University Press).

Hennessy, P. (2000) *The Prime Minister* (Allen Lane).

Jackson, N. (2003) 'The Blair Style – Presidential, Bilateral or Trilateral Government?', *Talking Politics*, vol. 15.3, January 2003.

Kampfner, J. (2003) *Blair's Wars* (Free Press).

Kavanagh, D. (2001) 'Tony Blair as Prime Minister', *Politics Review*, vol. 11.1, September 2001.

McNaughton, N. (1999) *The Prime Minister and Cabinet Government* (Hodder).

McNaughton, N. (2002) 'Prime Ministerial Government', *Talking Politics*, September 2002.

Moran, M. (2005) *Politics and Governance in the UK* (Palgrave).

Rentoul, J. (2001) *Tony Blair, Prime Minister* (Time Warner).

Rose, R. (2001) *The Prime Minister in a Shrinking World* (Polity Press).

Seldon, A. (ed.) (2001) *The Blair Effect* (Little, Brown).

Seldon, A. (2004) *Blair* (Free Press).

CHAPTER 9

The Core Executive

Contents

Overview

The concept of a 'core executive' has been developed as a way to broaden and expand analysis of executive power beyond discussions based around the traditional Cabinet/Prime Minister relationship. Building on the issues raised in the previous chapters regarding the nature of prime ministerial power and style, we can now go on to expand and conclude our analysis to include a detailed discussion on the issue of the core executive in British politics. By including this debate into our broad study of executive power we will be more able to arrive at detailed conclusions as to the true nature of executive power as it exists in the early years of the twenty-first century.

Key issues to be covered in this chapter

- Definitions and theories of the nature of core executives
- The nature of Prime Minister/civil servant relationships in a core executive and the changing context of prime ministerial influence
- How the core executive works and how it has evolved
- Criticisms of the core executive

The core executive: definitions

At its most basic, the term 'core executive' refers to the key institutions at the very centre of government. The core executive consists of a large and variable number of players that includes the Prime Minister, the Cabinet and its committees, the Prime Minister's Office and the Cabinet Office. It also includes large co-ordinating departments, such as the government's law officers, the security and intelligence services and the Treasury.

One of the first steps towards constructing a core executive model was produced in 1990 in a very influential article by Dunleavy and Rhodes that appeared in the journal *Public Administration*.[1] The article provides us with a detailed definition that stresses the importance of the concept of the core executive and also provides a good starting point from which to study, it. The two writers set the scene for our study of the core executive by giving us a clear definition:

- The core executive refers to all the organisations and procedures that co-ordinate central government and function as final arbiters of conflict between different parts of the government machine.
- The core executive is the heart of the machine and covers a complex web of institutions, networks and practices surrounding the Prime Minister, Cabinet, cabinet committees and their official counterparts, and less formalised ministerial 'clubs' or meetings, bilateral negotiations and interdepartmental committees.
- The core executive also includes co-ordinating departments. These include: the Cabinet Office, the Treasury, the Foreign Office, the law officers and security and intelligence services.

In explaining the importance of his definition, Rhodes argues that the label 'cabinet government' as the overarching term for some of these institutions and practices is both inadequate and confusing because it does not describe accurately the effective mechanisms for achieving co-ordination. The core executive argument does not rehabilitate the Cabinet in any way from the criticisms we have already levelled at it. As Rhodes has stressed in a later work: 'At best, it is contentious and, at worst, seriously misleading to assert the primacy of the Cabinet among organisations and mechanisms at the heart of the machine.'[2]

The core executive: a useful model

As a working model, the core executive is useful to all students and observers of the British political system as it extends analysis beyond the axis of Cabinet and Prime Minister and acknowledges the existence of a larger and less fixed network of power relationships that embraces Westminster, Whitehall and key players outside of these two traditional key areas of power and influence. By embracing and engaging with the concept of a core executive, we allow ourselves a different dimension on the traditional triangular debate of prime ministerial, presidential and cabinet power.

As we have already suggested, the concept of the core executive has been developed by political scientists in response to the endlessly frustrating debate on the issue of prime ministerial versus cabinet government. Rather than see the Cabinet and Prime Minister engaged in a seemingly endless struggle for political supremacy, the idea of a core executive offers us the idea that, in fact, both institutions are embedded in a network of relations with other influential bodies and people. It is the peak, or apex, of this power network that is labelled the 'core executive'.

We have already seen how writers such as Dunleavy and Rhodes have focused on the notion of a core executive as a way out of the impasse on prime ministerial versus cabinet government. Ignited initially by Bagehot in the 1860s and thereafter stoked occasionally by influential works, such as a Richard Crossman's 1960s introduction to Bagehot, and later works such as the highly influential 'British Cabinet' by John Mackintosh[3], the debate has rumbled on in its current form for the best part of fifty years. At the centre of the core executive model is the belief that that the Prime Minister versus Cabinet argument no longer fits the reality of modern politics. There are two key reasons why this is the case:

- The focus on Prime Minister and Cabinet is too narrow and therefore ignores the range of institutions and players within the core executive that have a central role in the policy-making process.
- The traditional debate is based on a misunderstanding. Past observers have misjudged and misinterpreted the connections between the various actors and institutions within the core executive

and have therefore failed to recognise that the operation of the core executive is not about the Prime Minister commanding players but about building alliances, exchanging resources and adapting to prevailing circumstances. More recently, Rhodes has argued that the traditional debate is a product of academic focus on Westminster and Whitehall, where the Prime Minister is 'indeed prime'.[4]

The debate around the notion of a core executive has been further developed in recent years by writers such as Richards, Smith and Marsh.[5] The central argument remains: power belongs neither to the Cabinet nor to the Prime Minister. Instead, political power is fluid. It develops in the complex web of relationships within central government and, if we are truly to understand power in the core executive, then we need to be completely analytical in our approach. If we are to summarise the arguments of one particular writer on this issue, we are able to define the core executive approach in nine key points:[6]

- It is wrong to assume that the Prime Minister and the Cabinet have all the **resources** of central government. All the various individuals and groups in the core executive bring something to the table; all of them have resources at their disposal that can make them formidable opponents of the Prime Minister and his/her Cabinet.
- The second part of the approach is all about the goals of every player in the core. If any one person or any group is to achieve their goals, then they must co-operate to exchange resources. It is virtually impossible for any one player in the core executive to make policy separately.
- If we approach the debate in terms of prime ministerial, presidential or cabinet government, we are dealing with flawed concepts that are irrelevant. The reason for this is that power in the core executive is based on **dependence**, not **command**. This means that the key players are locked into the system in such a way that none of them can entirely command or direct the system; they all depend on one another to ensure that the system can actually work.
- The concept of dependence is crucially important to understanding the core executive. What we need to identify are the **structures of dependence**: these are the routes and processes that everyone in the core uses in order to exchange resources with one another.

- Observers claim that these structures of independence are based on **networks** within the core that overlap one another. Occasionally, this can be a problem for the smooth running of the core because these networks can often be based on loose and informal structures that can lead to **fragmentation**, where not everyone is entirely clear of the roles and responsibilities of all the other players. This fragmentation and uncertainty over territory and responsibility can sometimes lead to conflict.

- Some of the key players in the core are what we refer to as **resource rich**: this means that they do not need to struggle for attention or resources in the core. A good example of a current key player who is resource rich would be Tony Blair. As we have already seen, as Prime Minister he has made substantial changes to the organisation of Number 10 (in particular the Cabinet Office) which have left him even more resource rich than is usually the case for Prime Ministers. Another example would be Gordon Brown. As Chancellor, Brown has the multitude of resources of the Treasury machine at his disposal as well as, in the words of one political journalist, 'sovereignty in the economics sphere' following the infamous Granita restaurant meal in May 1994.[7] The other big players in the Cabinet must also be considered resource rich. In the core executive, however, even these powerful individuals with access to significant resources are dependent on other players to achieve their goals. Government that works through a core executive is therefore all about the construction of alliances and mutually beneficial relationships rather than about command.

- All the players in a core executive operate within a clearly structured arena or territory. By this we mean that everyone has a place in an executive that is organised and arranged around clearly defined structures. This approach is the opposite of those traditional approaches that have tended to overemphasise the significance of personality.

- Personality cannot change the nature and form of the core executive. Prime Ministers, officials and ministers are bound by the structures of external organisation and have a fairly clear idea of the rules by which the government 'game' is played. They will also be aware of the structure and nature of the external institutions and players which whom they must interact. Strong personalities may therefore come and go but the essential nature of the core executive will remain the same.

- The context of any political or economic situation will decide the degree of dependence that the players in the core will enjoy. Actors will become more or less dependent in line with these contexts. Gordon Brown, for instance, has managed a relatively successful economy since becoming Chancellor in 1997. This economic success, coupled with the resources we spoke of earlier (and the apparent 'deal' with Blair) give him considerable political freedom. Similarly, a Prime Minister buoyed up by election victories and large majorities will enjoy significant room for manoeuvre and independence. In the face of an economic downturn and/or a very poor election showing, however, both Prime Minister and Chancellor would be required to become much more dependent on support from the other key players in the core, especially from the rest of the Cabinet.

The core executive is, for all the reasons listed above, fragmented and very difficult to co-ordinate. It should also be clear that it is the relationships between the key players, rather than the personalities of those involved, that frame the nature of the workings of central government. For those academics who study the core executive in detail, it is the relationships we have already referred to that make the prime ministerial/presidential-government debate redundant. This debate, they argue, asks the wrong questions and actually moves us further away from any clear understanding of how central government really works. Smith (in Holliday) sets out the six key questions which students of central government should be asking when they analyse the relationships in the core.[8] We can summarise them in the following box:

Having established what is a central fact regarding the crucial nature of relationships in the core, we can now move on to look at them in much more detail.

The relationship of the key players in the core

The Prime Minister

We should remind ourselves that, whatever model we choose to use in our analysis of the machinery of government, the Prime Minister

Box 9.1 Relations in the core: the key questions

The Prime Minister and cabinet ministers	• How would you define the relationships that Prime Ministers develop with colleagues? • How are Prime Ministers and ministers able to build alliances with other players in the core? • How quickly, why and with what effect do these alliances change?
Whitehall	• How would you define the networks established between the Prime Minister, ministers and senior civil servants? • How far does Whitehall structure the nature of the relationships between ministers and civil servants?
The wider political context	• How are all the relationships in the core influenced by events in the wider political context?

is the head of the government and, as such, has major resources at his or her disposal. In Chapter 5 we examined the nature of prime ministerial power in some detail; we also noted the constraints on this power. We can summarise the powers and resources of the Prime Minister as follows:

- Authority – from various sources
- Political support from cabinet colleagues and the majority of back-benchers
- Support from the wider party that he/she leads
- Support from the electorate who have voted the government into power
- A substantially strengthened Prime Minister's Office
- The growth of bilateral policy making
- The wide powers of patronage

All these powers and resources are available to the Prime Minister through the office. The constraints on this power are not insignificant and are explained in some detail in Chapter 5. It will be useful to summarise them here as:

- Cabinet
- Party
- Outside world

The Prime Minister, therefore, has powers and resources and these are subject to constraints. Nevertheless, the Prime Minister is expected to make choices about policy and the management of government even though the contexts in which these decisions will be made are varying and unpredictable as are the resources available to the Prime Minister and to all the other players in the core. As you can see, we have deliberately left the personality of the Prime Minister out of the equation on the grounds that personality may well have an impact on the structure of government but style is shaped predominantly by their dependencies and the wider political context. At this point, some writers argue that it is best to strip from the Prime Minister all notions of personality and attempt to see the holder of the office as primarily and an institution of government.

Ministers

Ministers occupy a somewhat different world. The main arena for a minister will always be the department. Ministerial resources may include:

- Political support from the Prime Minister and the rest of the Cabinet
- The strength and organisation of the department
- The specific policy knowledge the minister may possess
- The policy networks into which the minister has been taken or gained entry to
- In some cases, significant policy success will make ministers valuable allies to other players who have greater resource dependencies

In terms of constraints, ministers are faced with the rules and structures of their departments, the various values and institutions central to their particular areas of policy, and other colleagues in the Cabinet. Norton has argued that, while ministers are powerful figures in government, they are subject to 'remarkable' constraints that frequently make it difficult for us to make sense of their role in British government.[9] Like the Prime Minister, cabinet ministers will also find themselves making decisions about policy within these varying contexts, structures and resource dependencies, all of which are constantly shifting and subject to unpredictable outside factors.

The relationship between ministers and civil servants is particularly complex, and a wide selection of models is available to anyone who wishes to look at this in greater detail. One of these models – the power-dependency model – is particularly useful to us as part of this discussion and we should summarise the key points here before we proceed.

In short, the power-dependency model suggests an environment in which ministers have to negotiate with other actors to achieve desired outcomes. Even this brief one-sentence description should suffice to establish the value to students of the model of the core executive.

The model was developed by Rhodes, initially to analyse the complex nature of centre–local relations.[10] There are two central propositions to grasp in order to develop our understanding of power dependency.

- The model is based on the belief that any organisation is dependent on other organisations for resources. The Prime Minister, for instance, has considerable resources at his or her disposal, *but never enough*. Number 10 cannot supply everything, and the Prime Minister will often be dependent on resources available only through government departments. The same applies to ministers, who are almost entirely dependent on their departments and on civil servants to provide policy advice and then to carry out their decisions. Even the civil servants themselves will then need 'their' minister to fight an effective battle with the Treasury so that the department will continue to be resourced adequately. This is not to say that conflict dominates the relationships in any or all of the examples we have used. In a government secured by large majorities and sound economic management, the relationship will most likely be one of co-operation.

- The second proposition in the model is that organisations must exchange resources to achieve their goals. For a body to be effective, it cannot operate exclusively of others, and players within the body will require the co-operation of others in the system if they are to achieve their goals. In other words, there is a dependence on others. To achieve this, alliances must be created and resources traded.

The model recognises the central feature of the effective core executive: there may well be a group or individual player who can dominate the relationships in government but those relationships will change as players fight for position. If we accept the power-dependency model (not just to illuminate the position of ministers but also to illustrate the completeness of the core executive) then we are accepting a complex and less hierarchical process than those models that see ministers primarily as the agents of Prime Ministers or civil servants. This model, therefore, sits along the principal-agent model – where ministers are agents of the Prime Minister or of civil servants – and the **baronial model** which suggests ministers have their own policy territories complete with castles and courts around which they fight or build alliances to get their own way.

Civil servants

Whitehall and its officials occupy a different territory to that of the elected politicians. According to Smith, they 'operate in a context where the rules of the game are essentially set by a constitution that the officials maintain through their actions and their beliefs'.[11] In this view, the Constitution and its 'enveloping' myths set the limits of official behaviour, to the extent that civil servants are much more the continuing 'bearers' of the structure of government than the ministers.

To illustrate his point, Smith uses the example of a change of **permanent secretary** in one of the main government departments. The impact of such change is relatively small. In suggesting this, we are not saying that the civil servants are powerless or do not function (there is far too much evidence to suggest otherwise) but that the territory of their action is very different from that of the politicians. So, the territory and the context are significant for all the key players. Recent reports and inquiries – notably the Scott Report and the Hutton Inquiry Report – have revealed the considerable freedom that civil servants enjoy as they seek to interpret their freedom of man-oeuvre while attempting to maintain their constitutional loyalty to the ministers. The flexibility here is considerable given that the Constitution is 'largely mythical' and it is left to the civil servants to untangle and interpret the myth.

In terms of the 'resources' available to the officials, we can also see some key differences from those we have listed against the politicians:

- Permanence, as opposed to the dark clouds of election and reshuffle that hover over the heads of ministers.
- Knowledge though still mainly generalists as far as the actual policy area of the department is concerned, the civil servants will have a far greater understanding of how that department functions and how it relates to other areas of the government. This 'Whitehall Network' is a considerable resource based on permanence and shared civil-service values, and has been developed and nurtured over a long time. Politicians are rarely able to construct similar networks themselves.
- Control over information. Numerous narratives in contemporary studies and biographies that deal with the minister/civil servant relationship illustrate this resource. *The Alan Clark Diaries* offer a particularly good illustration of how officials attempt to 'ambush' and control the flow of information to ministers, while Ian Lang's description of the response of a senior civil servant to his simple request for a piece of paper is a classic of the genre. 'The Civil Servant returned, holding a single sheet of paper "Like a dead rat".'

The Civil Service is also subject to considerable constraints. The focus on delivery, the development of agencies, and the introduction of management rhetoric and technique have had an impact as have the decreasing role in policy formulation and the large-scale cuts to the size and staffing of Whitehall.

To summarise this section on the relationships between key players, we should focus on four key points in relation to the structure and workings of the core executive:

- The Prime Minister, cabinet ministers and civil servants function in different structures and territories from one another.

- The territory of the civil servants is very different from that occupied by politicians.
- These individual players have at their disposal resources that are not available to other players.
- Personalities may be important in these relationships but they are not the key factors in the working of the core executive.

Now that we have examined the core executive in terms of key definitions, individuals and relationships, we can move on to look at how the modern core executive actually functions.

How the core executive works

It is important to note that the core executive is not fixed. Unlike a static and unchanging structure, the core executive is fluid and changing according to circumstances and the wider political context. For instance, the military and defence situations at any given time will have a significant impact on the structure of the core. In recent years, there has been a number of opportunities to attempt to piece together this shifting core as a result of the various military commitments that Britain has been involved in, especially under Tony Blair. It is possible to state that, in these circumstances, the top British military leaders will find themselves entering the inner circles of the core only to pass out again once a particular military operation has been resolved. The likelihood is that British military commanders will have been very close to the core since 2001 and the subsequent 'war on terrorism'. Similarly, the terrorist attacks on London in the summer of 2005 will have brought senior officials into the core from a number of anti-terrorist agencies. In a book referred to earlier, John Kampfner explains the workings of COBRA, the government's emergency committee (which gets its name because of the meeting's location in Cabinet Office Briefing Room A), when news began to reach London of the attacks on the World Trade Center in September 2001. Kampfner's account is doubly interesting: not only does it reveal the actual shifts and movements around and within the core, it also provides a neat example of Blair's use of the bilateral meeting by explaining how, before the meeting began at 5.30 p.m., Blair had already had individual meetings with the key ministers – Gordon Brown, Jack

Straw, Geoff Hoon, David Blunkett, Stephen Byers and Alan Milburn, the Health Secretary – who then attended the full COBRA session, each bringing with him a senior civil servant. In the brief meeting (it lasted just over thirty minutes), short presentations were made by the various security and intelligence agencies on the key focus of domestic security. It is interesting to note, however, that, after the initial meeting, COBRA met three more times that month while the full Cabinet met only once. Kampfner makes the point that 'Blair's inner circle was all that mattered' while Number 10 referred to Blair as 'seeing people when necessary'. We will come back to this particular point later in the chapter when we consider the criticisms of the idea of a core executive.

The meetings of COBRA that took place in September 2001 had a very different format from those that had taken place the last time the committee had needed to sit. The earlier meetings had taken place the previous year when protesters had successfully disrupted the distribution of fuel throughout Britain. On that occasion, COBRA had not worked particularly well, and changes had been made. The 'tables for two', each with a lap-top computer, and the bank of televisions, each showing the various twenty-four-hour news channels, were a new innovation, as was the row of sound-proofed telephone booths.

COBRA is obviously an example of the core at its most dramatic. Other examples from the Blair era that illustrate this flow of people into and out of the core include the foot-and-mouth epidemic, the various developments associated with devolution and constitutional reform, and the ongoing issue of Britain's relationship with the Europeans Union, especially in the aftermath of the Constitution debacle during early summer 2005.

Various metaphors and diagrams have been constructed in recent years in an attempt to explain how the core executive 'looks' and how it functions. Some of these attempts simply add confusion to the topic. The standard 'block' diagram, that shows the key players locked by joining arrows as they bargain and co-operate with one another, cannot hope to show the full complexity of the core. The more detailed diagram offered by Pyper and Robins is better,[12] but again tends to focus on the key players in terms of their relationships rather than attempting to illustrate the fluidity and complexity of the changing political circumstances and contexts that we have outlined above.

An effective way of visualising the core executive is to think of the central government machinery as a top-of-the-range compact disc player with multidisc facility. The machine itself represents the permanent or semipermanent players in the government. We already know that these include the Prime Minister, the Cabinet, and civil servants alongside other key players with important resources, such as the cabinet committees, law officers and security and intelligence services. Now, think of each of the CDs in the machine as representing a particular political issue or crisis. Because the central machinery rarely has the luxury of dealing with one issue or crisis at a time, it is able to shuffle between the 'discs' as it attempts to juggle priorities, make alliances and gauge the resources that are both available and in short supply. Some discs may spend a long time in the machine and will be subject to long periods of play. Others will be taken from the sorter after a brief period and not be 'played' again. As the 'discs' pass in and out of the machine, so do some of the key players for that particular issue, be they senior veterinary scientists in the case of foot-and-mouth or experts in Balkan affairs as in the case of the war in Kosovo. At any particular time, it is difficult to say with precision who is 'in' and who is 'out', another reminder that the core executive model is open to some criticism.

The core executive – 1945 to 1980
Another useful way of examining the core executive is to set out how the central government machinery used to function. Between the end of World War II and the start of the 1980s, it was possible to make several basic observations about the key features of the core. These are summarised in Box 9.2.

The core executive – 1980 to present
Since 1980, it has been possible to argue that the defining features of the post-war core executive have shifted significantly. The reasons for this shift have been documented in detail elsewhere and we do not need to go into them in depth here. It is important to note, however, that the shift did occur at the same time as a prolonged period of almost one-party government in the United Kingdom that came to have a very distinctive and different ideological view from those governments that had been in power previously. These internal pressures therefore combined with significant external pressures in such a way

Box 9.2 The core executive: 1940s to1980s

The post-war expansion of central government and the increased role of the state demanded that the core executive developed a particular set of features.

The state had to assume a high degree of central control. This was largely owing to the post-war policies of nationalisation and the introduction of the welfare state.

The increased role of the state required the government to develop a vast bureaucratic machine.

The post-war state and government had to be prepared to undertake an interventionist approach to society and social issues. This was often on a large scale.

Key economic groups (including trade unions) were incorporated into the policy-making process.

Politicians and officials conducted their business with a high degree of consensus as to their respective roles in policy and decision making. This spirit of consensus even extended to the relationship between parties where there was a general agreement on the management of a mixed economy, defence and the welfare state.

as to change fundamentally the key features of the core executive. Smith argues that there are six key changes to note.[13]

- There is no longer the tendency to provide detailed intervention. This has been replaced by a general nudge towards the setting of the overall direction of policy rather than the detail.
- The management of government has changed. It is now 'decentralised and delayered' rather than focusing on bureaucratic management.
- The business of government is now less about the directing of state bureaucracies and more to do with the management of policy and delivery networks.

- The public sector has shrunk considerably. As a result, there is much less of it for the core executive to manage.
- Economic groups are now effectively excluded from the policy-making process.
- Consensus has largely had its day. While on the one hand, it is now possible to bemoan the general lack of 'difference' between the main parties, this is certainly not the case in the relationship between officials and politicians.

In Chapter 6 we outlined the nature of the bureaucracy surrounding the Prime Minister and, in particular, the changes that have been made to the Prime Minister's Office and the Cabinet Office. These changes to important 'structural resources' of Number 10 have considerably strengthened the hand of the Prime Minister as the key player in the core executive, and have given Blair in particular a greater role in the formulation and co-ordination of policy. Conversely, the resources available to civil servants have been diminished, a fact that is particularly noticeable when ministerial/official resources are compared and when we remind ourselves of the constraints listed in the previous section.

The modern core executive now functions in a world where the established structures of dependence have changed. Four key points may be summarised from Thomas that illustrate these changes.[14]

- The core executive has now become more dependent on international organisations than was previously the case. Membership of the European Union is a good example of how some areas of decision-making have moved outside the core.
- Ministers are now more dependent on the resource-rich Prime Minister than they were before.
- New means of exchanging resources and building alliances have arisen between external agencies and government departments.
- The Treasury is increasingly dependent on departments to deliver resources even though the Prime Minister and the Treasury manage, on the whole, to have more advantages than disadvantages over the other players and institutions within the core. It is important to remember that everyone else in the core needs to access the resources at the disposal of Number 10 and the Treasury.

Writers such as Smith and Pryce have gone on to argue that the modern core executive is now more concerned with governance than government. If the core executive was ever sovereign (and there isn't a great deal of evidence to say that it was) then it certainly is no longer. Instead, the core executive is at the centre of a complex network of competing organisations, none of which it can directly control. These competing organisations include:

- Privatised utilities
- Agencies
- International bodies
- The European Union
- Quangos
- Voluntary agencies

In dealing with the various parts of this complex network, the centre of the core executive – Prime Minister and Treasury – find themselves exchanging resources and building alliances with individual players. These competing individuals are as much a part of the changing contexts of politics as are all the other players, yet all may react and make choices in different ways. Under these circumstances, the best the core executive can do is to concentrate on **indirect control** through contracts, regulations and the markets. Government has therefore given up on any attempts to use nationalisation and bureaucratisation as means of direct control. For those involved the consequences have been twofold:

- On the one hand, government has been made easier simply because there is now less for it to do, less to be responsible for.
- On the other hand, government has been made more difficult because the complex network we have been discussing now has access to the control panel of power once lorded over almost exclusively by the core executive.

Having pointed out the limitations that modern politics places on the core executive, it is still worth mentioning that that executive has major advantages over other players. It continues to be highly and effectively resourced. It can claim major resources of authority and legitimacy, and is able to control powerful financial resources. Finally, if all else fails, the core executive can always turn to the resources that allow it to deploy a range of legal and coercive measures. In other words, no one else can call in the armed forces, no one else can declare a state of emergency. In this sense, the core remains at the core with all the potential ability to utilise all the resources of the state that you would expect would accompany such power.

In the course of our overview of the core executive, we have suggested that there is a number of criticisms of the model. This chapter will conclude by setting out these criticisms.

Criticisms of the core executive

The nature of the core executive, as we have explained it here, leads to a number of key questions. The first question raise issues about the actual composition of this core at the heart of government while the second asks searching questions about its effectiveness.

Does the core executive exist?

We should consider the questions below as a starting point:

- Who should be included in the core executive: Chief Whips? chairs of the back-bench committees in Parliament? representatives of insider pressure groups? In short, how are we to analyse efficiently a structure that has no fixed place and no fixed and certain membership?
- What about the role of cabinet committees in the core – are all of them to be considered as 'core' or are some more 'core' than others?
- What about the modern Prime Minister's Office and Cabinet Office? We have already made the case that both bodies have experienced significant reform and change in recent years. Does this mean that all the individuals involved in these offices are therefore to be considered members of the core?

Given these questions, and the fluid nature of the core executive which changes according to circumstances, it is hardly surprising that some writers have questioned whether there is such a thing as the core executive at all.[20] It is certainly the case that some of the examples and debates which have been outlined in this chapter may be used to question the concept of a core executive. Notwithstanding the constraints listed against the principal players, we are still left with an 'inner' core of Prime Minister and Cabinet with an ever-changing cast of 'outer' players circling around them. It would be possible to argue that we end at the place we tried to leave, which was essentially a description of prime ministerial and cabinet government.

If the core executive does exist, how effective is it?

There was a time before Blair when some commentators appeared to bemoan the absence of a single executive that could provide policy leadership and a coherent control of the machinery of government. For one observer, writing in the *Guardian* in 1997, there existed a 'hole in the centre of government' where policy remained mostly in the hands of the departments, thus undermining the constitutional conventions of collective decision-making and accountability.[15] Critics were also pointing to the weakness of co-ordination and strategic direction at the core of British politics, and a desperate need to end the 'short-termism' that had characterised most post-war governments. To achieve these aims structurally, some reformers argued that inner cabinets needed to be formed that would be tasked with the direction of government. During the same period it was possible to read regular calls for the formal establishment of a Prime Minister's Department.

For other observers, many of them still wary of the trends set in motion during the Thatcher period (others continuing to deliver the same warning they had been refining since the 1960s), what the British executive definitely did not need was more centralisation and inner strategic control. Far better, they argued, to cut back the power and secrecy of the government; far better perhaps to limit the powers of the Prime Minister (especially patronage) and move towards a much more decentralised and accountable executive. As one group of writers argued, Blair came to power and almost immediately began to face, Janus-like, in the directions of both the competing demands outlined above.[16] This position can be neatly explained in the box below, and supporters and detractors of the Blair governments will be able to make their particular cases by using the evidence of the two columns:

It remains the case that any core executive is essentially the sum of all the contexts and players that we have discussed in this chapter.

Box 9.3   More or less government? Blair and the core executive

Responses by Blair to the 'hole at the centre of government' argument	Responses by Blair to 'too much power at the centre of government' argument
• Considerable reforms to the Prime Minister's Office and Cabinet Office – a 'Prime Minister's Department in all but name'. • Units established to concentrate on strategy and delivery. • Emphasis on 'joined-up government'. • Greater use of task forces. • Stronger control over ministers' activities through the Strategic Communications Unit. • Stronger political control over the government bureaucracy. • Promotion and placement of 'Blair people' to key ministerial and non-ministerial positions.	• Incorporation of the European Convention on Human Rights. • Freedom of Information Act. • Handing power to set interest rates to the Bank of England's Monetary Policy Committee. • Devolved assemblies in Scotland, Wales and Ireland. • Support for (though not popular with the electorate) regional assemblies. • Elected mayor for London, London Assembly. • Some modernisation of local government. • Continuance of devolved power in the NHS.

It is also important to remind ourselves that the core executive remains a well-resourced and formidable political machine, and that effectiveness or otherwise will be decided in the short term by the electorate and the players themselves and in the long term by political historians.

Concluding points

For a model constructed to challenge the prime ministerial or cabinet government debate, it is interesting that our discussion ends with a consideration of the Prime Minister in order to make a larger point about the core executive. Yes, the resources of the Prime Minister have increased, yet this does not necessarily mean that the power of the Prime Minister has increased accordingly. Matthew Flinders, writing in the *Politics Review* helps draw the strands of our discussion to a neat conclusion.[17]

- Decision-making is moving beyond the core executive.
- Government is enmeshed in a range of international and global interdependencies, which limits the executive's scope for action in many policy areas.
- Continued and greater European integration, devolution, and government reform make co-ordinating policy much more difficult.
- Many players are involved in policy-making; the Prime Minister cannot control all of them.
- The executive acts in an environment that is 'dense with constraints, but the strength and vigour of these limitations depend on the specific context of each situation'.
- As the British state becomes more fragmented and diffuse, the executive needs to develop new steering and control mechanisms and is reluctant to do anything that might fetter the power it has.

••

✔ What you should have learnt from reading this chapter

We began this chapter by looking at key definitions of the core executive. To remind you, the term 'core executive' refers to the key institutions at the very centre of government. The core executive consists of a large and variable number of players that includes the Prime Minister, the Cabinet and its committees, the Prime Minister's Office and the Cabinet Office. It also includes large co-ordinating departments such as the government's law officers, the security and intelligence services and the Treasury. Having established a basic definition, we went on to discuss the origins of the model and looked at the theories of writers such as Rhodes and Smith.

Having established our definition, we then went on to discuss the uses of the core executive as a model. We noted the availability of the model as an alternative to the prime ministerial/cabinet-government type of debate and, we hope, recognised that, in choosing to focus on the core executive, we were developing themes already set out in some detail in earlier chapters. Having looked at how the model could then be applied to the British system of government, we discussed some key concepts that are central to the debate, such as 'resource' and 'resource dependence'. You can check your understanding of these key phrases in the glossary below.

Our discussion of the core executive has also included detailed comparisons of the key relationships between the Prime Minister, cabinet ministers and civil servants, and also provided you with an overview of how the core 'works' and what criticisms have been made of the model.

🔎 Glossary of key terms

Baronial model A model of ministers that sees them in policy territories, complete with castles and courtiers around which they fight or build alliances to get their way. Developed by Norton (2004)

COBRA The government's emergency committee.

Command A political style of strong leadership and control from the centre.

Core executive Key institutions at the very centre of government. The core executive consists of a large and variable number of players which includes the Prime Minister, the Cabinet and its committees, the Prime Minister's Office and the Cabinet Office. It also includes large co-ordinating departments, such as the government's law officers, the security and intelligence services and the Treasury.

Dependence Where one player in the core executive depends on the support and/or resources of other players to achieve his or her aims.

Fragmentation Used to describe a political system where the key players are unsure of their roles and responsibilities, and where structures are beginning to fracture.

Indirect control An attempt to use political power to control a situation indirectly through agencies or institutiuons.

Permanent secretary Senior civil servant in a government department.

Power-dependency model A power model in which ministers have to negotiate with other players in the core to achieve their ambitions.

Principal-agent model Where all ministers are agents of the Prime Minister and/or civil servants.

Resources/resource-rich Resources in the tangible sense (information, funding) and also used to refer to authority, influence, legitimacy etc. Resource-rich refers to players with access to substantial resources, i.e., Prime Minister and Chancellor.

Short termism A political strategy which ignores long-term policy planning in return for the quick electoral fix of immediate and 'quick-result' short-term decisions.

Structures of dependence The networks and complex web of relationships in the core executive whereby alliances are formed and resources are traded.

❓ Likely examination questions

Short questions

Describe what is meant by the term 'core executive'.

Describe why the model of the 'core executive' was formulated.

Briefly describe the nature of the relationship between the three key players in the core executive.

Describe the central features of the post-war core executive.

Explain why the workings and structure of the core executive have changed since the early 1980s.

Essay questions

To what extent do discussions on the core executive reveal certain weaknesses at the heart of the British system of government?

How far would you agree with the suggestion that the Prime Minister has more power now than ever before?

'The Prime Minister can no longer control the actions of all those involved in the core executive.' How far do you agree?

Discuss the suggestion that the core executive model does little more than reframe the prime minister/cabinet-government debate.

Critically discuss the core executive model as an effective way of analysing key political relationships.

Revision task

Take a packet of index cards and make yourself a deck of revision cards on the core executive. Begin with three cards: Prime Minister, cabinet ministers and civil servants, and then write brief sentences on other cards to link them together. Gradually build up the number of cards you have until you feel you have covered all the aspects of the core executive as they have been dealt with in this chapter. Clear a space on a table and start to place the cards down randomly one at a time. The idea of this revision task is slowly to arrange the cards until they are laid out on the table in some logical way that helps you remember all the key theories and arguments associated with this topic.

Helpful websites

The usual government websites will be useful:

www.number10.gov.uk/

The 10 Downing Street website.

www.direct.gov.uk/

Particularly useful for department and Civil Service links.

www.cabinetoffice.gov.uk/

Very good for detailed studies of the central government machinery.

www.civilservice.gov.uk

Suggestions for further reading

Flinders, M. (2003) 'Controlling the Executive', *Politics Review*, vol. 13.1, 2003.

Foley, M. (1993) *The Rise of the British Presidency* (Manchester University Press).

Kampfner, J. (2003) *Blair's Wars* (Free Press).

Norton, P. (2004) 'Ministers, Departments and Civil Servants', *Talking Politics*, ed. B. Jones, 2004.

Pryce, S. (1997) *Presidentialising the Premiership* (Macmillan).

Pyper, R. and Robins, L. (1995) *Governing the UK in the 1990s* (Macmillan).

Rhodes, R. A. W. (1995) *Prime Minister, Cabinet and Core Executive* (Macmillan).

Rhodes, R. A. W. (2005) Presidents, Barons, Court Politics and Tony Blair (PSA).

Smith, M. J. (2000) 'The Core Executive', *Politics Review*, vol. 10.1, 2000.

Smith, M. J., Richards, D. and Marsh, D. (2000) *The Changing Role of Central Government Departments* (Macmillan).

Thomas, G. P. (1998) *Prime Minister and Cabinet Today* (Manchester University Press).

CHAPTER 10

Conclusion: The Prime Minister, Cabinet and Synoptic Skills

Contents

Overview

This brief concluding chapter will bring together the key arguments of
the book and will suggest ways in which students may wish to use the
other books in this series to undertake a detailed synoptic overview of the
Prime Minister and Cabinet in terms of other aspects of the British political
system and perhaps even to consider using the information and arguments
here as a starting point for detailed comparative study.

Key issues covered in this book

- The British system of cabinet government has experienced considerable
  change in recent years.
- It is possible, if using traditional definitions as a starting point, to announce
  the 'death' of cabinet government.
- Structural reforms and changes in Downing Street have considerably
  increased the potential power of the Prime Minister.
- It is possible to detect aspects of the Prime Minister's power and role that
  now make the post increasingly 'presidential'.
- The increasingly complex web of relationships and networks in which the
  Prime Minister and Cabinet now operate suggests that the central
  government machinery should be viewed as a 'core executive' rather than
  as the traditional idea of co-ordinated and effective cabinet government.

Synoptic study

Synoptic study is now a key theme of A-level and undergraduate politics programmes. The concept of synoptic study is essentially the drawing together of all the knowledge and understanding you have developed throughout the duration of a complete course on government and politics. The purpose of synoptic study is two fold:

• From a purely examination board point of view, synoptic study is designed to encourage students to see their study of politics as a 'whole' rather than as separate and unconnected units.
• Politics is by its very nature a 'synoptic' subject. It is impossible fully to make sense of an individual aspect of a politics course if you do not have an understanding of the wider context of your study. It is impossible, for instance, to appreciate fully the true nature of Parliament if you concentrate your study exclusively on the House of Commons and ignore the House of Lords. Equally, you will not develop a full understanding of the true nature of British government if you study only the Prime Minister and Cabinet. As we have tried to show throughout this book, context is everything.

To develop your understanding of the Prime Minister and Cabinet in more detail you should now go on to place the key themes in the wider context of British government and politics. The following suggestions may be useful:

Pressure groups – what connections and links can you detect between the proliferation of pressure groups in the United Kingdom and the current nature of Prime Minister and Cabinet?

The judiciary – how often do the Prime Minister and Cabinet find themselves at odds with the judiciary, and why?

Elections and parties – without elections and parties, the Prime Minister and Cabinet would not be in power. What are the connections and links between these themes? What impact did the 2005 general election have on the Prime Minister and Cabinet?

Devolution – Blair has carried out reforms in this area that may well have taken power away from him. Why? What other implications has devolution had for the Prime Minister and Cabinet?

America – studying comparative politics is a very good way to develop your synoptic skills. What are the similarities and differences between the American and British cabinets? Is the Prime Minister really a presidential figure?

Europe and the European Union – what are the implications for the Prime Minister and Cabinet of continued UK membership of the EU? Is the Cabinet broadly for or against further integration within the EU? Why is the Euro a controversial issue in the Blair Cabinet?

Religion and morality – how far have the domestic and foreign policies of Tony Blair been conditioned by religious and moral considerations? To what extent has Blair been able to use his position to deliver solutions to populist campaigns such as Live 8?

War on terror – are the Cabinet and the Prime Minister coping? What are the implications of the war on terror for the British government?

Blair and Brown – what are the implications for government and party in the relationship between Tony Blair and Gordon Brown? Will the Labour Party choose a 'coronation' of Brown or will there be other challenges? To what extent will Brown maintain the style of government developed by Blair?

Reading

The following books will help you with your synoptic studies:

Cohen, N. (2003) *Pretty Straight Guys* (Faber).

Naughtie, J. (2005) *The Accidental American: Blair and the Presidency* (Macmillan).

Rawnsley, A. (2001) *Servants of the People* (Penguin).

Stephens, P. (2004) *Price of Leadership* (Politico's).

Stothard, P. (2003) *Thirty Days – A Month at the Heart of Blair's War* (HarperCollins).

References by chapter

Chapter 1

1 Bagehot, W. (1867) *The English Constitution*, 1963 print with an introduction by Richard Cressman (Fontana).
2 Kingdom, J. (1999) *Government and Politics in Britain* (Polity Press).
3 Kingdom, J. (1999) *Government and Politics in Britain* (Polity Press).

Chapter 2

1 Jones, B. and Kavanagh, D. (1998) *British Politics Today*, 6th edn (Manchester University Press).
2 Jones, B. and Kavanagh, D. (1998) *British Politics Today*, 6th edn (Manchester University Press).
3 Rose, R. (2001) *The Prime Minister in a Shrinking World* (Polity Press).

Chapter 3

1 Brady, C. and Catterall, P. (2000) 'Inside the Engine Room: Assessing Cabinet Committees', *Talking Politics*, vol. 12.3, spring 2000.
2 Budge, I. (ed.) (2000) *New British Politics* (Longman).
3 Burch, M. and Halliday, I. (1996) *The British Cabinet System* (Prentice Hall).
4 Seldon, A. (2004) *Blair* (Free Press).
5 Naughtie, J. (2002) *The Rivals* (Fourth Estate).
6 Mandelson, P. (2002) *The Blair Revolution Revisited* (Politicos).
7 Brady, C. and Catterall, P. (2000) 'Inside the Engine Room: Assessing Cabinet Committees', *Talking Politics*, vol. 12.3, spring 2000.
8 *The Times*, July 1998.
9 Rentoul, J. (2001) *Tony Blair: Prime Minister* (Time Warner).
10 Hennessy, P. (1998) 'The Blair Style of Government', *Government and Opposition*, winter 1997–8.

Chapter 4

1 Gay, O. and Powell, T. (2004) 'The Collective Responsibility of Ministers', House of Commons Research Paper, November 2004, 04/82.
2 Benn, T. (1981) *Arguments for Democracy* (Penguin).
3 Quoted in Gay, O. and Powell, T. (2004) 'The Collective Responsibility of Ministers', House of Commons Research Paper, November 2004, 04/82.
4 Dorey, P. (1991) 'Cabinet Committees', *Talking Politics*, vol. 4.1, autumn 1991.
5 Gay, O. and Powell, T. (2004) 'The Collective Responsibility of Ministers', House of Commons Research Paper, November 2004, 04/82.
6 Hennessy, P. (2004) 'Systems Failure at Heart of Government', *Independent*, 16 July 2004.
7 Rathbone, M. (2003) 'The British Cabinet', *Talking Politics*, vol. 16.1, September 2003.
8 Rentoul, J. (2001) *Tony Blair: Prime Minister* (Time Warner).
9 Mowlam, M. (2002) *Momentum: The Struggle for Peace, Politics and the People* (Hodder).

Chapter 5

1 Kampfner, J. (2003) *Blair's Wars* (Free Press).
2 Rentoul, J. (2001) *Tony Blair, Prime Minister* (Time Warner).
3 McNaughton, N. (1999) *The Prime Minister and Cabinet Government* (Hodder).
4 Foley, M. (2000) The British Presidency (Manchester University Press).
5 Johnson, R. W. (1990) 'The President has Landed', *New Statesman*, 30 November 1990.
6 Burch, M. and Halliday, I. (1996) *The British Cabinet System* (Prentice Hall).
7 Rentoul, J. (2001) *Tony Blair: Prime Minister* (Time Warner).
8 Rose, R. (2001) *The Prime Minister in a Shrinking World* (Polity Press).

Chapter 6

1 Milne, K. (1998) 'The Policy Unit', *New Statesman*, July 1998.
2 James, S. (1992) *British Cabinet Government* (Routledge).

3   Rose, R. (2001) *The Prime Minister in a Shrinking World* (Polity Press).
4   Kavanagh, D. (2001) 'Tony Blair as Prime Minister', *Politics Review*, vol. 11.1, September 2001.
5   Hennessy, P. (2002) 'The Blair Government in Historical Perspective', *History Today*, January 2002.
6   Burch and Halliday (1996) The British Cabinet System (Prentice Hall).

Chapter 7

1   Rose, R. (2001) *The Prime Minister in a Shrinking World* (Polity Press).
2   Norton, P. (1987) 'Prime Ministerial Power: Framework for Analysis', *Teaching Politics*, vol. 16.3, September 1987.
3   Heywood, A. (1997) *Politics* (Macmillan).
4   Norton, P. (1987) 'Prime Ministerial Power: Framework for Analysis', *Teaching Politics*, vol. 16.3, September 1987.
5   Mandelson, P. and Liddle, R. (1996) *The Blair Revolution* (Politico's).
6   Fairclough, N. (2000) *New Labour, New Language?* (Routledge).
7   Kavanagh, D. (2001) 'Blair as Prime Minister', *Politics Review*, vol. 11.1, September 2001.
8   Judt, T., *Tony Blair, A Man of Moral Certainty* (March 2003) http://www.pbs.org/(Public Broadcasting Service).
9   Smith, C., *Tony Blair, A Man of Moral Certainty* (March 2003) http://www.pbs.org/(Public Broadcasting Service).
10 McNaughton, N. (1999) *The Prime Minister and Cabinet Government* (Hodder).

Chapter 8

1   Moran, M. (2005) *Politics and Governance in the UK* (Palgrave).
2   Seldon, A. (ed.) (2001) *The Blair Effect* (Little, Brown).
3   McNaughton, N. (1999) *The Prime Minister and Cabinet Government* (Hodder).
4   Jackson, N. (2003) 'The Blair Style – Presidential, Bilateral or Trilateral Government?', *Talking Politics*, vol. 15.3, January 2003.
5   Hennessy, P. (2002) 'The Blair Government in Historical Perspective' (*History Today*, January 2002).
6   Burch, M. and Halliday, I. (1996) *The British Cabinet System* (Prentice Hall).

7 Quoted in McNaughton, N. (1999) *The Prime Minister and Cabinet Government* (Hodder); and 'Prime Ministerial Government', *Talking Politics*, September 2002.

8 Kavanagh, D. (2001) 'Tony Blair as Prime Minister', *Politics Review*, vol. 11.1, September 2001.

9 Foley, M. (2000) *The British Presidency* (Manchester University Press).

Chapter 9

1 Rhodes, R. A. W. (1995) *Prime Minister, Cabinet and Core Executive* (Macmillan).

2 Rhodes, R. A. W. (2005) *Presidents, Barons, Court Politics and Tony Blair* (PSA).

3 Mackintosh, J. (1962) *The British Cabinet* (Stevens).

4 Rhodes, R. A. W. (2005) *Presidents, Barons, Court Politics and Tony Blair* (PSA).

5 Smith, M. J., Richards, D. and Marsh, D. (2000) *The Changing Role of Central Government Departments* (Macmillan).

6 Smith, M. J. (2000) 'The Core Executive', *Politics Review*, vol. 10.1, 2000.

7 White, M. (2003) *The Guardian*, 6 June 2003.

8 Smith, M. J., Richards, D. and Marsh, D. (2000) *The Changing Role of Central Government Departments* (Macmillan).

9 Norton, P. (2004) 'Ministers, Departments and Civil Servants', *Talking Politics*, ed. B. Jones, 2004.

10 Rhodes, R. A. W. (2005) *Presidents, Barons, Court Politics and Tony Blair* (PSA).

11 Smith, M. J., Richards, D. and Marsh, D. (2000) *The Changing Role of Central Government Departments* (Macmillan).

12 Pyper, R. and Robins, L. (1995) *Governing the UK in the 1990s* (Macmillan).

13 Smith, M. J., Richards, D. and Marsh, D. (2000) *The Changing Role of Central Government Departments* (Macmillan).

14 Thomas, G. P. (1998) *Prime Minister and Cabinet Today* (Manchester University Press).

15 Bogdanor, V. *The Guardian*, 4 June 1997.

16 Smith, M. J., Richards, D. and Marsh, D. (2000) *The Changing Role of Central Government Departments* (Macmillan).

17 Flinders, M. (2003) 'Controlling the Executive', *Politics Review*, vol. 13.1, 2003

Index

Bold indicates that the term is defined